THE END OF ME OLD CIGAR
and
JILL AND JACK

JOHN OSBORNE

The End of Me Old Cigar

a play

and

Jill and Jack

a play for television

FABER AND FABER LTD

3 Queen Square London

First published in 1975
by Faber and Faber Limited
3 Queen Square London WC1
Printed in Great Britain
by Latimer Trend & Company Ltd Plymouth
All rights reserved

ISBN 0 571 10856 3 (Hard bound edition)
ISBN 0 571 10857 1 (Faber Paperbacks)

The End of Me Old Cigar

CAST

STELLA SHRIFT

LETITIA PANGBORN

MRS. ISOBEL SANDS

JOG FIENBERG

LADY GWEN MITCHELSON

LADY REGINE FRIMLEY

LEONARD GRIMTHORPE

ROBERT BIGLEY

STRATFORD WEST

FREDERICK BLACK

JOHN STEWKES, M.P.

ASHLEY WITHERS

SMASH DEEL

STAN ('MR.' FRIMLEY)

WAIN

RACHEL, THE COUNTESS OF BLEAK

The play was first performed at Greenwich Theatre on 16th January 1975. The cast was as follows:

LADY REGINE FRIMLEY	Rachel Roberts
STAN	Neil Johnston
WAIN	Toby Salaman
STELLA SHRIFT	Sheila Ballantine
LETITIA PANGBORN	Angela Galbraith
MRS. ISOBEL SANDS	Jill Bennett
LADY GWEN MITCHELSON	Jasmina Hilton
JOG FIENBERG	Marty Cruickshank
RACHEL, THE COUNTESS OF BLEAK	Joanna Lumley
LEONARD GRIMTHORPE	Keith Barron
SMASH DEEL	Roderic Leigh
FREDERICK BLACK	Ian Milton
STRATFORD WEST	Kenneth Macgarvie
JOHN STEWKES, M.P.	Charles Kinross
ASHLEY WITHERS	John Grillo
ROBERT BIGLEY	Mike Lucas

Directed by Max Stafford Clark

ACT ONE

SCENE: FRIMLEY HOUSE

The sitting-room of large country house. It should be very large. Jacobean, perhaps, with Knole sofas. Anyway, whatever period, furnished in the most circumspect taste and careful-careless luxury, reflecting a little on the extravagant nature of its owner, LADY REGINE FRIMLEY. *There are huge, elaborate mirrors everywhere. She is lying back, listening to the final trio of* Der Rosenkavalier. *As she listens, enraptured, her 'husband'* STAN, *(she is a widow) sits reading the* Melody Maker *and various racing papers. She is about late thirties, slightly older than he. She is a most attractive woman, finely but comfortably dressed. He is rather the sort of man who poses in the nude for magazines or manages pop groups or boutiques. Presently, but not for a while, she brings the trio to an end by turning off the record player. Pause.*

STAN: What you turn it off for? Any tips for the Gold Cup?

REGINE: Lady Be Good.

STAN: Get on. What's his form? Can't even find it here. Oh, yes. . . . If the going's wet.

REGINE: One of the stewards told me. He put a hundred pounds on for me—to win, of course. And I've had a tip from the weather bureau . . .

'Es send die mehreren Dinge auf der Welt,
so dass sie ein's nicht glauben tät,
wenn man sie möcht erzählen hor'n.
Alleinig wer's erlebt, der glaubt daran und
weiss nicht wie . . .
Da steht der Bub, und da steh'ich,
und mit dem fremden Mädel dort
wird er so glücklich sein, als wie halt Männer
das Glücklichsein verstehen.'

STAN: That's Kraut, I know. What is it? What you were
   listening to?
REGINE: Three women, singing together, right? One, older, the
   Marschallin, the other two younger. The Marschallin is
   renouncing the boy she loves. But as you watch this great
   cascade of love spurring out like the thunderous spray of a
   vast waterfall of heartbreak, comes this *sound*. But you
   know it's three *women*. The love of women, the love of
   woman for woman, the love of love itself and life continuing
   and replenishing the earth. Only they the true fruit and
   proper multiplies. The fruit of a tree yielding seed. Listen,
   if you can tear yourself away from Smash Deel. (*She turns
   up the record player again.*) This is the Marschallin, the older
   one, watching her young lover with his betrothed: (*Pause.*)
   'Most things in this world are unbelievable when you hear
   about them.
   But when they happen to you, you believe them, and
   don't know why—
   There stands the boy and here I stand, and with that
   strange girl
   He will be as happy as any man knows how to be . . .'
   (*She turns it off.*) Isn't that sublime?
STAN: Yes.
REGINE: Vulgar and sublime as only woman can achieve. She
   renounces the thing she loves the most: Octavian, orders,
   her life, her heart, to go to his bride.
STAN: Was it written by a man?
REGINE: Two men, overbearing Viennese pigs. Strauss and Von
   Hofmannsthal.
STAN: What, the Blue Danube geezer? He *could* have been a
   woman.
REGINE: Richard not Johann. He *was* a soppy man. You should
   read their letters to each other.
STAN: What, were they pouves?
REGINE: No. It's a lesson of two men trying to collaborate.
STAN: Like Morecambe and Wise?
REGINE: Do you know what he said, forty years later when
   some American soldiers broke into his house at the end of

the war? They demanded: 'Who are you?' And he replied:
'I am the author of *Der Rosenkavalier*!'

STAN: That must have stumped them. Who's this Rosy
Cavalier? How'd he treat *his* wife?

REGINE: Abominably.

STAN: But don't they, the audience, know it's a bird in drag?

REGINE: Of course they do, dolt! But they don't *feel* it. They
feel them as three women, resplendent in their bodies
and star-pointing female voices.

STAN: Didn't Shakespeare do that?

REGINE: But everyone knows Rosalind and Viola are an oafish
Elizabethan's hairy idea of what they want a woman to be:
poor imitation men. I'll take you to see it one day.

STAN: Thanks.

REGINE: I often wonder if Mozart wasn't a woman.

STAN: Wasn't he called Wolfgang? Good name for a group.
Not bad—Wolfgang . . . (*He pronounces it* WOLF.)

REGINE: His sister, his Constanze. *He* understood women. Ach,
Constanze! All his women were like sisters. Look what fools
men are: Almaviva pillaging and bullying for the privilege
of his enslaved maidenheads; Figaro himself; Papageno—
pathetic; Leperello, notching up the count of brutal
seductions on his master's belted so-called manhood. The
belt of young girl's slavery and gullibility; and Don
Giovanni, that *arch* pretender! Squalid rides into town,
cowboy cocksman, penile gangster. He got *his* St.
Valentine's Day all right, bootlegging his crabs and disease
and sad seed all over civilization. They've all got their
St. Valentine's Day coming to them, this blight of the
world's Casanovas. A quick, sharp burst from all over the
earth; from every girl from the North Side, the South
Side, the West Side, the East Side.

STAN: Thought St. Valentine's Day was for lovers. Why, I
sent you a card once.

REGINE: Very sweet of you, darling. But misguided in these
times.

STAN: I see Smash Deel's number two in the charts.

REGINE: Yes, he mustn't start to slide. He's coming here today.

STAN: What—Smash? Cor! Can I see him?

REGINE: You will. You'll be busy with your camera and tapes.

STAN: No, not when he's on the *job*. Afterwards. Perhaps when he's finished? I could have a chat with him? About his work and that?

REGINE: *When* he's had his this and that with the girls—which I suspect won't be much of either this or that. His trousers are too tight for his padding not to cast doubt on that holy of holies.

STAN: Think he's bent?

REGINE: Just straight nothing-in-particular. Well, we shall see. About the only sensible lines in 'Man-God's Genesis' I really like are the ones, how do they go: 'And I will put enmity between their seed and her seed; (*her* seed, note)— it shall bruise their head, and thou shalt bruise his heel.' Well, his maybe along with a lot of other bruised heels and there'll be no bruised heads among *us*. As for bruised heels, you should be on yours getting down to the bank with all last night's stuff and put it in the box.

STAN: Right. I just want to put something on the three-fifteen—

REGINE: Well, hurry up with it. What horse?

STAN: Mr. Spats.

REGINE: Not a chance.

STAN: Who says so?

REGINE: That trainer who was here last night. Captain Addison.

STAN: Who'd he say then?

REGINE: Periwinkle II.

STAN: Periwinkle II. Sure?

REGINE: Look with my retention, I could be one of those middle-aged matrons who fictionalize their marriages with endless streams of consciousness.

STAN: Eh?

REGINE: And are *you* sure you got the stuff on him?

STAN: Oh, sure. He's quite an old stallion himself. Got through four of the girls. In three-quarters of an hour. I thought the film was running out.

REGINE: Good. Sounds like our bank manager. He was quite a

14

bull—under those striped trousers. By the way, I can't find my key.

STAN: What?

REGINE: To the bank box, stupid.

STAN: Never mind. I've got mine.

REGINE: I want mine. Order another. I'm not sure these joint accounts are much good.

STAN: Depends on who makes the most bread. Man usually.

REGINE: These are valuables, evidence, bombshells; the key to revolution! When I finally walk into that bank for the deposit boxes, it'll be like Lenin arriving at the Finland Station.

STAN: Ms. Lenin, more like. Anyway, you hate unloading all that piles of stuff.

(WAIN, *the butler, appears.*)

REGINE: Yes, Wain.

WAIN: Miss Shrift is here, m'lady.

REGINE: Send her in. She'll get impatient and I'll find myself in her column on Monday.

(WAIN *goes.*)

'Come off it, Lady Germaine-Frimley Pankhurst. As far as women's rights are concerned, you're just a titled show-off who needs a good, properly paid job of work like the rest of us ordinary nine-to-five housewives. Do your good works like the rest of us try to—even with the kids.' Ten thousand quid a year *she* gets for that. Still, she's got a following—what they call hard-hitting popularity.

(STELLA SHRIFT *is ushered in by* WAIN. *She is about forty, rather over-dressed, 'hard-hitting' indeed and irrevocably, irremediably in a Fleet Street Rose convention.*)

REGINE: Stella, darling! What a relief. You *are* the first to arrive. I wanted to explain some things.

STELLA: Always on time. Have to be in my job. No time to stand and stare. Don't get copy that way. Oh, who's got 'hard-hitting popularity'?

REGINE: The Vicar's wife, oddly enough. She wants to sack the choir-boys and use girls. She says the boys just pick their noses and play with themselves under their sweet little surplices. She says they're so stained the church can't keep up with the laundry bills.

STELLA: I'll bet. Mind if I use that? Might be worth an inch or two.

REGINE: Appropriate phrase. Oh, yes, she's very militant.

STELLA: I hate those angelic little, well-brushed dirty little devils. Church propaganda for the innocence of man in his youth. Two of them jumped on me and ripped my gym-slip off and all but raped me.

REGINE: Poor girl. Well, get on, Stan. Oh, this is my er——

STELLA: Hullo, Mr.—er—Frimley.

STAN: Way out, Miss Shrift.

STELLA: Way out? Does he mean hanging out?

REGINE: He's always catching up with last year's *Melody Maker*. Well, get on, Stan. And don't forget that key.

STAN: Right. See you, Miss Shrift.

STELLA: I'll be breathless.

(*He goes out.*)

REGINE: Drink or tea?

STELLA: Nothing, thanks. I may not stay long.

REGINE: I think you will. Sit down, darling. Anywhere. You can go, Wain. Keep an eye out for the other guests.

(*He goes.*)

STELLA: I may not be able to stay, as I say. I might look in at the Hunt Ball Fashion Show. Sure to be a drag but the readers like a bit of how-the-other-half-lives. Especially the upper classes or their hunt followers and hangers-on fooling about with champagne; old-clothes couturiers turning the place into a flunkey's bazaar for nancy photographers and the general debs' drugs.

REGINE: I said the Vicar's wife was militant but not on *your* scale of power and influence. Don't they—I mean those sweaty men in El Vino, or whatever it is, call you the Black Fleet Street Rose?

STELLA: Not to my *face*. Now, what do you want from me? Not a polite country-house guest.

REGINE: What I think we'd both like.

STELLA: Which is what?

16

REGINE: I think *I* will have a drink. Do you mind?

STELLA: Be your guest.

REGINE: Rather a long stay.

STELLA: Not too long, I hope. My stuff's short and to the point. That's my house style.

(REGINE *fixes herself a drink while* STELLA *cases the room.*)

REGINE: Now, Stella ... do you mind if I call you Stella?

STELLA: Thousands do. Quite a place you have here. Stables and grooms too, I see.

REGINE: I've always liked to live in the manner I'm accustomed— especially in the country.

STELLA: Were you always accustomed to such gracious living?

REGINE: Not on anything like this scale. But I always followed country pursuits eagerly.

STELLA: I'm sure. And got pursued for it.

REGINE: And then my late husband loved the country. He was Joint Master.

STELLA: Quite a nice cut off the joint all round. I shouldn't think Stan goes in for these—pursuits. Or girl grooms?

REGINE (STELLA *couldn't put* her *down*): He's always busy. He shouts a bit, goes to the races, a bit of photography—not for magazines——

STELLA: No. Home movies?

REGINE: Yes. Quite recently that. Oh, and he's very interested in pop. He managed a group for a while.

STELLA: Name?

REGINE: The Wheelwrights was one. Then I think it was The Vendetta.

STELLA: Doesn't ring a bell.

REGINE: Not much with me either. But he's very keen on 'young people'. I can't say I am myself. I don't think youth is its own reward any more than virtue. Being young in itself is hardly an achievement. Any more than having brown hair. I never liked young people when I was a 'young people' myself. But then he likes clichés, which is what young people are, of course.

STELLA: You couldn't read newspapers without them.

REGINE: Nobody would understand them then, would they?

But I'm afraid Stan is a bit of a cliché himself, wide open to popular fashion. I suppose people who *are* clichés must be certain to learn others, even in their speech. He doesn't talk a lot but when he does I often don't understand him at all. He even uses ones he doesn't understand.

STELLA: Like?

REGINE: Oh, he understands the usual ones: like—funky; cool it—I think that's out—; bad trips; being in some sort of 'scene'—sounds like a part in a play to me; having hang-ups—he has lots of those I believe; chicks, birds, calling everyone 'baby'; saying 'fucking' because he doesn't know any other adjectives—or hardly; chart-buster; he's picked up some he doesn't grasp at all from some of the girls with social consciences, in particular. Oh, you know the sort of thing: street action groups; committee jargon; lobbying the council; even 'growing resentment'—you might read that in *The Times* even; play communities, play centres, play groups, centres for; centres of *all* kinds from 'pig bashing' to 'aggro' and 'agit-prop'; playgrounds, parks; talking about his groups as if they were the Amadeus Quartet . . .

STELLA: Seems to me you don't like many things. Including Stan.

REGINE: Oh, but I do. I don't believe in hiding one's malice. I like women and some men; sex now and then, preferably in private; horses——

STELLA: Naturally.

REGINE: —some dogs, most cats; champagne, chip butties, Guinness; oysters, gulls' eggs; opera, stand-up comics—not drag acts though; some older homosexuals; Jane Austen not Conrad; a certain religiosity if it's comic enough; silver—you might like to see my collection; motor bikes, roller-skating and, still, I'm afraid, Monte Carlo; rock and roll if it's the older, more primitive sort; Hell's Angels. Oh, I can't think . . .

STELLA: A picture emerges.

REGINE: Oh, hate crosswords, chess and bridge and all the people who like them.

18

STELLA: You seem to like mirrors too, I see.

REGINE: Adore them. Even when I look awful, which is most of the time.

STELLA: For what you see *in* them? Or through them? Come, Lady Frimley, you didn't invite me all the way down here to give an interview. We're not each other's scene.

REGINE: I think we *might* be.

STELLA: Look, let's get down to it. I may still have to go to the huntin', shootin', fashion show. Is it true what I hear that you run a call-girls' establishment for randy, big-name weekenders?

REGINE: Yes.

STELLA: Right. Now what do you want?

REGINE: Don't you want what Evelyn Waugh called a scoop?

STELLA: Listen, Lady Frimley, I know you think you're something of a two-way personality smart-ass. But I don't think you're a fool. Some sort of kooky revolutionary, classic English eccentric—which you couldn't be. Oh, yes, I've looked around about you.

REGINE: Naturally. How professional of you.

STELLA: Don't play games with me. I know them all and the rules, even the ones to break. All right, we all know you're a phoney. Name, background, publishers, the lot. You're not thirty-eight and you're a Jewish girl from Hackney with a goodish plastic surgeon. And your name is Myra Steinitz.

REGINE: Right. Absolutely. Every detail. Nice of you not to mention my other marriages. Still, they're fairly common knowledge. No, you see, I am something of a cliché myself.

STELLA: So then: what's the set up here?

REGINE: Well, it's not quite what you imagine. I think it's a trifle more sophisticated, both in function and intention. It *is* what you say—in a few column inches that is to say. Yes, the mirrors *are* two way. What insights into life 'as it is really lived' the profession of journalism gives a young girl—as time goes on. I have been running this 'place', if you like, for quite some time. Quite long enough for me,

and if as you say, there are already rumours about it where
you come from, it's high time to pack up the operation
and plan for the next and most important stage.

STELLA: And that is?

REGINE: Oh, some sort of frolicsome revolution or simple old
shit hitting the world's fan. I have run this 'establishment',
if that's the word, to have enticed almost every man in
England.

STELLA: I don't believe it. Men always cover up. And in their
numbers there's safety. How ever many have you got?
You know there are scoops and scoops; the law of libel.

REGINE: English libel. An old dog in his corner of the world.
There's the *world* press. German magazines, French ones,
Dutch, Swedish television companies, America. Russia.
I've got quite a missile here, as an American general said
to me once.

STELLA: Go on.

REGINE: This makes Watergate three-day cricket for baboons.
I've got film, thousands of MILES of it. And with what a
cast. Well, all the obvious ones, I needn't tell you.
Parliament. I didn't know we had so many members.
Sorry, but it did seem more than six hundred. Judiciary,
of course. Press but enough and not more. Civil Service,
Armed Service. Royals. Footballers. Daft ones, gay ones,
rotten ones, distinguished. Oh yes, the Church, but they
don't count for much. Tapes, stills. Too much material,
of course. But used superbly. We can't make it so all-
embracing that everyone will yawn and get down to it
themselves. What we need is a superb team; team, yes,
of directors, Eisensteins, Orson Welleses, John Fords, to
put it all *together*. A sort of works of Shakespeare, Ivan
the Terrible in epic parts. How does it begin to strike you?

STELLA: Interesting.

REGINE: Remember. Think of us. Us. Women. Half the world.
That rocked the cradle could bring down the chop for all
time. Or long enough.

STELLA: As simple as that?

REGINE: As all discoveries of genius. Banally simple. Like

20

Leonardo, the wheel, iron weapons, the workers over-
throwing the *ancien régime*. And the *régime* is certainly
ancien, I'm sure you'd be the first to agree. Pure organisa-
tion. Apparently, again, too true for the words of even the
simple clichés of Stan. *I* recreate a very English cliché.
The Country Weekend. This is the Garsington of
Lechery—instead of Literature.

STELLA: Garsington?

REGINE: Garsington. It was the rather spinsterish, on all sides,
world of Ottoline Morrell. The world of Asquith, Keynes,
Duncan Grant, Virginia Woolf and Leonard, Lawrence——

STELLA: I know. I know. I don't just read newspapers, you know.

REGINE: All very respectable. Waspish witticism and music
and banjos and economics, flirtations and politics. People
can't flirt any more, can they? Pity; I enjoyed it once.
Saved you from all that thrashing about after and
perspiration and excuses and making calls from phone
boxes instead of your house. All quite different from your
mustachioed Edwardian adultery festivals and the Countess
of Warwick and bedroom keys and nightgowns and brandy-
port filled men slipping down those long cold corridors to
the heavy warmth of another's heaving feather four-poster.

STELLA: What have you got apart from thousands of miles of
unedited film and so on?

REGINE: Stars, you mean: oh, about a thousand of what used to
be called pillars of society, paragons of public life.

STELLA: Simple. You get the stars and the equipment. What
about the girls?

REGINE: Fresh picked. To them it doesn't matter. If they go
along with the principle, they've nothing to lose. *They're*
the heroes. They caught out the cancer. They'll be the
Provos of Womanhood all over the world.

STELLA: Maybe the *other* women won't buy it.

REGINE: They will. They'll have to. *You* know the way it's
going. And in such a short time. The star is in the firma-
ment. And it shines for *us*. The revolution *will* come.
Then we'll see. It'll find its Robespierre.

STELLA: And you its Danton?

REGINE: I've had a good life. I expect it to be better, for a while, at least.

STELLA: Where's all this vast production-script?

REGINE: In the bank vaults. Stan does that. He'll do anything for money. To him it's just a new cliché of history. Like 1066, 1789 or 1914—if he knows *them*.

(STELLA *pauses for thought*.)

Your presence. This must be the last weekend. You could be our link with 'the media' (cliché). Stay and see what you feel. It'll be more rewarding than the Hunt Ball Fashion Show.

STELLA (*intrigued now*): Tell me some more.

REGINE: This is the time to *strike*. We've got all we need. First, the girls will come. I'll brief you on them but I doubt you'll need it. The men you'll know about.

STELLA: So you think the soldier's pole is about to fall, pulled by *you*? You see, I do know my Shakespeare. I wonder. Like all these things. Some will like it. Some will hate it. There's one thing for certain, Regine. *There's no going back*.

REGINE: Welcome, my friend. As you say, there's no going back. We don't need to draw in any more if we don't want to. We're the girls' Jesuits. Give us a girl for the first of her grooming, her indoctrination, and I'll make her first a whore and then her whole self, her *self* for life. The prick is just where it is. The cunt is where the heart lies.

STELLA: Yes, all that shit about envy. Who'd envy *that*!

REGINE: Yes, it helps them in their endless romanticism about you. His balls are where his brains should be. That's why he used up what his mettle should be. Lyrical poetry, desire failing, laments for lost love, inaccessible troubadour mistresses without a servant. If only they knew how they sickened us with their schooldays, memories, endless, endless memories. Their peacock regimentals, their desperate fetishes and paltry pornography. Why? They are hollow, empty wooden horses all dressed up or undressed with nowhere in the universe to go. No Troy to infiltrate let alone *penetrate*. And what you said about envy. Envy! My God.

22

STELLA (*getting exhilarated*): No wonder the Victorians in their wisdom voted for fig leaves. David. Greek gods. Ugh! A schoolgirl's giggle round the V. and A. It was true aesthetic judgement, not a moral one.

REGINE: See it dangle, dingle dangle, jingle jangle in its usual petulant pendulance. A sorry, blue-veined pork sword looking like an unripe, yellowish Stilton. Lying against its horse-hair sack, wee bag, of a million million pestilent tadpoles looking for a muddy pool to rest in. Throbbing for all the world's distaste like a turkey's gobbling neck.

STELLA: No wonder they call it a 'gobble job'.

REGINE: Erect, well now, *that's* a sight, if they can get it up without your thumbs splitting and fingers enflamed with corns, more horn than they could ever manage with *that*. Erect as an Irish volunteer, blind, hopeless, eyeless in girls' Gaza. These footling frail inches of phallus, trying to ascend Everest like a Mick navvy without enough scaffolding.

STELLA: Perhaps *that's* what Disraeli meant by 'the greasy pole of politics'.

REGINE: Rather keen on poles, aren't they? Well, that flag won't fly much longer. It's coming down. In all its tatters and tyranny. *We* will be the mast, the mast, mast of woman, flying *our* flag. Greasy indeed! Mrs. Disraeli must have known the real truth behind that bit of front bench grandiloquence.

STELLA: And their awful *jokes*. You can imagine the stuff *I* have to listen to, Black Rose or not.

REGINE: Men invented bordellos, but women perfected the running of them.

STELLA: Like *you*! I *will* have a drink, after all. We'll drink to the weekend. To the revolution. To the scaffold agleam with male unreconstituting blood.

REGINE: Here's to us all.

STELLA (*relaxed now*): This joke, this journalist who called me Black Rose because I wasn't having his whisky head snoring on my breast. He told me this. Supposed to be sophisticated and male fun. Right? Ready?

REGINE: Ready. If you tell it well, I warn you, I might——

STELLA: They hate us because we can't *tell* jokes. Should be cut
like a good jacket. No joins. All that stuff. *Male* joke!
In this case Red-nosed Rose of Yorkshire. Bugsy meets
Louie. That's right. You see, I can tell it to you, like my
hairdresser. Bugsy says to Louie, say, Louie, you're looking
great. Great. Why it's years since I seen you. (*All in
gangster accent.*) Must be, what, eight—eight years. Yeah.
Long stretch. Say, where you living now? Florida. Great.
Miami Beach. Suits you. You look great. Great. Say,
whatever happened to that little broad—er, chick—girl you
were so keen on? What was her name? Rochelle. That's
right. Great kid. Gee, Louie, you're looking great. Say,
whatever happened to—er her, Rochelle. . . . I *married*
her. . . . Married her, married her, but that's great,
Louie. Really great. Say, how is she, Louie. . . . She's
dead. (How'm I doing?)

REGINE: Great.

STELLA: Dead! But, Louie, that's terrible, that's awful! Gee,
Louie. . . . What'd, what she die of . . .? CRABS . . .
Crabs! Jesus Christ, Louie, people don't die of CRABS . . .
They do if they give 'em to me. (*Actually her cigar, George
Raft imitation was quite good.*)

REGINE: I *told* you I'd laugh at one of *your* jokes. Even at one
of—those. The point is there's a General Amin in man
bursting, brown or white, to get out. 'Ah'm a good marks-
man.' So he can make twelve piccaninnies.

STELLA: All that rigidity. The fact is men don't want to die so
much they won't be born, so foetus themselves up in music
halls, clubs, regiments and pubs. Do you know what that
Yorkshire git said to me when he knew he wasn't going to
get it and was too pissed to remember where he'd left it?
He said, as if he were Voltaire, Morality is the child of
imagination, which is why women don't have it. That we'd
had more leisure than most to paint, sing, play the piano,
write poetry, verses, novels, music. What did we get: the
Brontës and the Ivy Benson Band. That not women
invented steam and God but US!

24

REGINE: How ignorant. (*Slightly sending up* STELLA'*s new fervour.*)

STELLA: Barefoot and Pregnant. Even sweet-natured Chekhov said women didn't have a baby every *day*. Just every year. Fable about Barefoot and poorly shod. I don't think sweet Doctor Chekhov would have bought you any shoes at all. As your cliché book would say, Marriage needs re-phrasing.

REGINE: We're in total agreement. But don't you see that's the point. We all are. To us. To us Women.

STELLA: Right.

REGINE: To us.

STELLA: To us.

REGINE (*toast*): The aim, the aim is *not* social equality, no, it's not that, it's social DISHARMONY. All they have is an inexhaustible crop of regrets. Regrets!

STELLA: *They* like the language of concealment. Not us.

REGINE: We're going to enjoy this, Stella. This is the barricades. At last.

STELLA: Barricades! Here we come! We're closing your border-line. Like Going into the E.E.C., it filled a long, unfelt want. Now we don't want *you*!

REGINE: You know that chap Aretino or something like that. I just went to Farley Road Secondary School till I was fourteen. Well, it seems this old character *laughed himself* to death at a dirty joke. *Just* like my old man. So did I nearly. Thank God *I* didn't. Think of all that money. Only time he made me laugh.
(*They both giggle.*)
We've got a whole spotlight of dignitaries and here come the last of the bombs. Lead 'em on!
(WAIN *comes in.*)

WAIN: Mrs. Pangborn is here, m'lady.

REGINE: Give me a minute and then show her in.

WAIN: Very well, m'lady.

STELLA: Letitia Pangborn?

REGINE: Who else? Publishers' parties and lays all round, grand Tory M.P. husband, writes books on the cookery of sex, travel (over- researched), popular biographies. Regrets, like so many, she hadn't been an actress and set the world alight without the benefit of rich husband, large ears and hungry little typewriter to feed for fame and a reputation for beauty *and* intellect . . .

STELLA: Wheel 'em on.

WAIN (*enters*): Mrs. Pangborn, m'lady.

(MRS. PANGBORN *is pretty, confident, about the same age as the rest.*)

REGINE: Darling! I'm so glad you're *first*. You know all the ropes. Only I've got a rather funny little lady coming next and I may have to sort her out a bit. You know Stella, don't you?

LETITIA: Yes. Hullo.

STELLA: It's all right. You've nothing to worry about from me.

REGINE: No. She's one of us.

STELLA: Yes. Not just an outside observer. A participant. A resistance worker. Not soon enough, alas. I could have helped.

REGINE: It was my one insight. It's nice to have *one*. Drink?

LETITIA: Thanks. Not before work. Who have you got for me?

REGINE: Stratford West.

LETITIA: Oh, not him. That awful, creepy show-biz journalist. Why do you always get me journalists?

REGINE: Sorry.

LETITIA: Don't be. I was just complaining.

REGINE: Well, poor Stratford can only get plastic starlets to roll in his garden before he goes back to the wife and kids in Ealing. Pretending he's been living it up—for the paper— to all hours. And he *wants* a bit of class and intellect. He can't spell 'existentialism' but he'll swoon when you bite it into his grizzled old ears.

LETITIA: Isn't it time we closed up shop? You must have enough to wreck the entire Western Civilization.

REGINE: That's exactly what we've agreed. With Stella.

LETITIA: Thank God. I'm sick to death of staring up at myself in the ceiling mirror. I almost fancy my husband. But the House is too busy having divisions these days.

REGINE: You can always go back to publishing.

LETITIA: That's like going back as an old girl when you were once Head Girl.

REGINE: How's the writing?

LETITIA: I wish you wouldn't ask silly questions to people like writers, Regine. You should know better. It's like asking a window cleaner 'How are the windows then?' It's the same as usual. It's all hours but I get it done. In spite of Tom and the children.

REGINE: Well, you *are* rich.

LETITIA: *He* is. Thank God.

REGINE: I've explained the set-up to Stella. She not only understands but she's right behind us.

LETITIA: Good. We'll need all the help we need. These men will think of *something*. That's what worries us.

STELLA: With your bottom in the air, your pants hanging down in a frightened animal way, it'll be difficult to think of anything. Privacy's never really been assaulted and brought down. They won't know what hit them or why anyone could do it to them. *Their* God will have cast *them* out. *We'll* be left laughing.

LETITIA: In Paradise? No men!

REGINE: We'll make our own paradise. Our own kind of men. And remake God's bad job on the whole unfortunate incident. We will multiply. We have already. That's what it meant.

LETITIA: I hope so. I can't *stay*, Regine. I'm sorry. Tom's wanting me on his constituency stint this weekend.

STELLA: Last time.

REGINE: As I said, I've this funny little woman——
(WAIN *comes in.*)

WAIN: Mrs. Sands, m'lady.

REGINE: Send her in.
(WAIN *goes out.*)
Be nice to her. She must be very nervous.
(WAIN *enters with* MRS. SANDS. *She is shrewd-looking but nervous. However, making a go of it. Late thirties. Quite attractive. Not startlingly dressed.* WAIN *goes out.*)

REGINE: Mrs. Sands! Isobel, right? Isobel, this is Letitia Pangborn, Stella Shrift—she shows no shrift and gives no favour—I expect you've heard of her?

ISOBEL: Yes. Of course.

(*They exchange the usual things and sit.*)

REGINE: Isobel, anything, no? Isobel, this won't be too difficult for you. These people are close friends and I've heard from many sources what an honest kind of character you are. We can be frank. If you want to change your mind at any time, of course you may. I'll understand. I just wanted someone quite honest, well, decent, who was intelligent and curious and in some distress but in control; objective but emotional, who would get in on this—just for once, and form her judgements for herself of what we have all created for ourselves.

ISOBEL: There's no danger of that. I shall stay as long as you need me.

REGINE: Wonderful. Well, to cases: there will be about five or six women here and about seven men. So some may have to do overtime.

STELLA: Jog. She's a sperm vampire.

REGINE: Could you tell me a bit more about yourself?

ISOBEL: Not much really. I've been married nearly twenty years. I've three teenage children who don't take notice of either of us much. They really scare both of us now and I suppose we avoid them most of the time and they us. . . . I feel young and I seem to have no future. Although, I *feel*, perhaps stupidly, it might be not new but *different*. I don't know . . .

REGINE: I know.

ISOBEL: I do know I reduce him to such despair and tedium, he dreads coming in and I dread the key in his lock.

REGINE: Don't worry. The stars are pointing for all of us. I've well, teamed you, if you don't mind the expression, with Leonard Grimthorpe.

ISOBEL: One's free. But for what. (*Pause.*) I'm sorry for him. And he for me. (*Pause.*) He really goes pale and damp with fear and irritation with me. I can watch it. It's like a boiling migraine. You need to put him to bed in the dark, alone as long as possible. While I sit and stare at nothing, well, our

28

house walls; the walls of our house.

REGINE: Isobel. Let me get you a drink. I have to be practical
I'm afraid. I have to be speedy and generalize because time
is pressing on us a bit. *Len Grimthorpe:* he's decided not
to be brilliant because he couldn't bear it. He really does,
I think, I think he does, he believes in the beauty of failure.
Not just as a literary throw-away for someone like Hindle
to seize on.

STELLA: Who's got *him*?

REGINE: You have.

STELLA: Oh, no. Not *two* journalists.

REGINE: Usual enough. Anyway, all this bedroom placement is
very difficult. *You* try it. You'll probably have Smash Deel
first.

STELLA: No. I think I'm resigning.

REGINE: It's only the once, Stella. And you are new. We've all
done our bit.

STELLA: What about Mrs. Sands?

REGINE: No, I don't think she could handle Smash Deel.

STELLA: Quick flick of the wrist.

REGINE: I think he'll take a lot more than that. He's a wrist
breaker.

ISOBEL: I'm very athletic. Yes, I know you're grinning. But I
don't need, I don't want to be protected.

REGINE: This is my placement. It took hours to work out and
I'm sticking to it. Otherwise, we'll all argue and be here
all night and no customers. (*To* ISOBEL:) Now Len is an
odd fish. But he can be fun. And he won't ask too much of
you. Because he expects so little. I see you're wearing tights.

ISOBEL: Oh, are they——?

REGINE: But the last time Len came he complained of someone—
I can't remember who—wearing tights. He said they were
for men not women. For male dancers and Shakespearian
actors. He couldn't stand that patchy triangle round the
centre. Definitely underwear, I'm afraid. I'll get it laid out
in your room. I know what he likes. Quite harmless and
dull. Totally *MALE*. Do *we* think of such things?

ISOBEL: Right. I'll remember. I wasn't sure.

29

REGINE: He's much more full of gaiety than he sounds. I think
you might get on. I can't quite think quite why I asked
him. He's not really famous. Sort of well known. For doing
nothing—much. But quite good at it.
(WAIN *enters.*)

WAIN: Lady Gwen Mitchelson and Miss Jog Fienberg.

REGINE: Two minutes, Wain. Show them the new conservatory.
(*He goes, nodding.*)
Lady Gwen: like me, a girl from Hackney. I knew her at
school. Another nibbling girl-actress who went to Hollywood
too late but brought it back to Weybridge or somewhere.
Lots of alimony from sweet, misguided ex-husband actor
who has given her two children, a mansion-by-Californian-
standards in Malibu. Lives off him and their accumulated
houses and pictures and furniture. Remarried title and some
money. Bad type for *us.* But ideal man bait. For the right
type. And there are plenty. Jog—yes, *Jog Fienberg*; U.S.
nutcase. Wants all men to have compulsory vasectomy
with or without the option of the death penalty. Now, she is
a cliché. Except that you won't believe her when you see
her. Don't listen, that's all. Above all, don't argue. Useful
because she does all the donkey work.
(JOG *and* LADY GWEN *enter.*)
Gwen, darling! Jog.
(*They fit her description.* GWEN *has clearly taken hours to
prepare herself.* JOG *is in jeans and sweater and badly, really
badly in need of a bath.*)

REGINE: You do make a quite splendid pair! I think you all
more or less know——
(*They go through the pantomime of introductions.*)
Drink? Ah, Coke for Jog.

GWEN: No, thanks.

REGINE: Not dieting again. It's so *oppressive.* Like your eye-
lashes and wigs. People who diet are like converts to warmed-
up religious beliefs. And your lovely rich husband, and
various children by which of them and your home? How
is your home? The Ranch Style one in Mill Hill? Or have
you moved?

GWEN: It's all great. So where are the guys?

REGINE: We're waiting for Rachel.

GWEN: Oh, the Countess of Bleak. She never really made it, did she? Couldn't act. Write. Anything. No good in the sack.

REGINE: Well, they do say that every cigar-smoking gentleman having lunch at the Black Rhinoceros has known the favours of both of you or either.

GWEN: Darling, if I didn't know you so well and had nothing better to do for an hour or so, I'd go straight back to London.

REGINE: Don't worry; this is the last of the weekends.

GWEN: Thank God! It takes so long to get here. And you know how suspicious Mitch gets.

REGINE: Next week is Bastille Day.

GWEN: What day? Here, I hope you're not going to go *too* far.

STELLA: We're all in this and you more than most. You compounded the system. With your make-up and Beverly Hills in Virginia Water; and film premières but no proper films; your alimony; your calculations; your shop-girl vanities. Just get on with being what you are and always have been; a prissy producer's tart with smart solicitors and accountants. You're not *unknown*, you know.

GWEN: Thanks. I don't need *you*.

STELLA: Watch it, you untalented trollop. I can get you eaten up. A threat like that from me, of all people, wouldn't intimidate little pussy. But it will *you*. Because, beneath all that British Beverly Hills, you're more of a cliché than you are and what you write about.

REGINE: And you Jog.

JOG: Is this the last one? I hope so. I can't stand another man, the sight of one. The mother-homemaker-secretary kind is still what they want, want, and they won't believe we're not. Who wants their prick rights? All laying down this crap. All stewing maleness and rhetoric. What are we, tits and no mind, to them? We are, we are the politics. The gags are better, they're better, not much but anything's better than what—they—call themselves—straights. Straight. What's

31

straight? In this world. Men? Straight. I'll never go again with any man. We all know what they end up *doing* to you! Sweet Jesus! Not *man*, Jesus! Give us, give us a woman for President! Is it possible? Couldn't it be? (*She weeps a little.*)

STELLA: You're not all that interesting, Jog.

JOG: Great. So tell me how uninteresting I am. I want a lover and it isn't a man and it isn't a woman. I'm a soldier, a fighter, I'm an academic, I'm educated middle-class American and you all, you English, look down from your sinking, stinking rat shit at us. . . . Help the woman who is obliged to work in any patriarchal, cultural set-up. A reunification of the reverence of the female principle. Give us the Goddess. Dig the Goddesses. Diana, Mary, Penelope. You have wasted us. *Wasted* us. We *are* your waste. Your effluent. Men and their things. Big deal. Big fucking deal. Let them do it to *them*selves. You're all a Big Deal. Protagonists. Tyrants. *We* are the killers now. Kill them. Kill the men. Before we do it. To ourselves. We're so scared. Kick out the fags too. Kill them all.

REGINE: Wain will get you some coffee.

JOG: What are we fucking well waiting for? You say I'm a cliché, don't you? Well, what do you think you are?

REGINE: The same as you. As all of us . . .
(*She rings the bell.* WAIN *enters.*)
Some coffee for Miss Fienberg. And anyone else.

WAIN: Yes, m'lady. The Countess of Bleak is here.

REGINE: Send her in at once. We're late.
(*He nods and goes out.*)
The Countess of Bleak. Another disjointed actress, married into the aristocracy from the usual disappointment and cupidity . . . I'm afraid you have to bait for the big fish with almost unspeakable morsels. If that's what gulls them. And it usually does.
(*They all look depressed in the extreme.*
WAIN *re-enters with the* COUNTESS OF BLEAK.)

WAIN: The Countess of Bleak.

REGINE: Darling. Anything? Sure, right, we'll start off. (*To*

WAIN:) Let the gentlemen in as they arrive. Oh, you know the batting order.

WAIN: Yes, m'lady.

REGINE: Well, how are the Bleaks?

RACHEL: Bloody mean and petty as ever for seven centuries.

REGINE: Now, I think we're all here. . . . You know why we're all here. Make bait and it's time to strike, haul up the nets and trawl in those wriggling creatures you've had to bear with in all this time. Jog, you've got, oh, I'm so confused now, I think you've drawn Smash Deel.

JOG: Kill him!

REGINE: And—I—think—Ashley Withers. Newspaper proprietor. Not Stella's but a well, BIG, little deal. Now, quick briefing: Stella, you've got Hindle. You know the score, you know him.

STELLA: Don't I just! They *all* do.

REGINE: Well, as I say, ladies, this will be our last weekend. I don't need to say much to you. Even our newcomer, Mrs. Sands, seems more than capable of holding her own—if you'll forgive the linguistic handstands of the good old English language. Even if some grandparents leapt off the boat from Omsk or Tomsk. I'll just add a few general things. As I say, Stella, you know Hindle, but he might stray, and they *do* sometimes, elsewhere——

STELLA: Hope so.

REGINE: Well, ladies, Hindle Nates is a famous ex-boy wonder from Oxford—I can't remember which college—who writes about almost anything for anyone and makes a great deal of money doing it. He has been trying to cultivate style ever since he was seen wearing lilac knickers and a top hat on Magdalen Bridge on his way to the Union reading Marx in a loud falsetto. He stunned the single-minded students, who've talked about it ever since and tickled some of the dons. He became a 'legend' in that city of dreaming spires and sure of soft jobs for its dud comics. He likes Wagner, anything American or clearly ephemeral, as well as danger-ously painful spanking. So watch for that. He hates the past, even yesterday, with almost pathological hatred.

33

And even today is a broken series of disappointments. You have to look like tomorrow's girl even if you feel like the forgotten or unfashionable decades of the century. So mind your bottoms, ladies. They can get very stripey and sore after half an hour with Hindle in the quest for his undergraduate glory. He writes unbelievably vindictive, incomprehensible, apparently erudite letters to obscure journals like the *Listener* which specialize in vindictiveness. So give him a bit of politics and literature. You don't need to say anything interesting or know who or what you're talking about. In fact, if you sound like Marilyn Monroe giving her views on Kierkegaard, he'll be perspiring with joy and discovery. A lot of what I say applies, in principle, to all our *other* guests. Their interests are all there to be titivated of whatever kind. But Hindle is quite a good example even if he's a bit over the usual intellectual top. As always, just drop a few names and he'll say something which he'll attribute to *you*. After all, he's grateful for the other services you're dealing out. . . . It never does any harm to pretend you like mostly plays by Negroes or Irishmen on the run for murder. Women's Lib tolerated, often welcomed by the 'bondage' artists. You can even pretend you're gay, which can spur some of them on. If you are indeed gay, it may be even helpful if it turns them off and it saves time and labour. They may, as often, think you're secretly longing, yes, here we go, to be *dominated*, yes, dominated by them, particularly if he's an established genius or today's idea of paradise and tomorrow's sexual garbage. You can offer him pot. Some will pretend to be in *that* scene. But most won't bother. You're safe with theatre chat because no one knows anything about it and cares less. Cinema is more dodgy because some of them are practically archivists and, anyway, it often digs deep into their grubby schoolboy consciousness. Say the Theatre is dead—as always—except the Fringe or Underground. You don't need to have *seen* any. *They* won't have seen any either. Or they'll have fallen asleep. Talk about non-happening happenings being the *ultimate* and so on. You don't have to *explain*. Just *say* it casually. Talk a lot of off-hand filth in between as if you were doing that brushing your glowing spring of hair from your clear fountainhead forehead. Just, oh, just be generally *charmless* is fairly good standard behaviour. But watch it if it misfires. Then, be gentle, loving, attentive. If you've got stubble in your armpits, say jolly things which will intrigue his running-down tape-recorder mind, desperately trying to freeze each new experience to release all the lost, shattered ones. So he'll tell you—a bit usually. Try not to actually bore him but let's simply hope he won't notice either ante or post coitum. It may be *triste est* quite often or just like getting up from a sauna and massage. There's always something he'll be interested in. Find it and he'll do the talking. Otherwise be enigmatic. Easiest thing in the world. Shut your mouth and look sulky. A few crass judgements may, on the other hand, make him feel good. Don't be *really* funny. That's poaching *his* rights. Oh, you can say—I'm sorry to be repetitive. *You* all know your stuff but I have to try and make you feel a bit enthusiastic about this *dismal* project. Remember it's the last time over that timeless top and then a New World waits for us! And we were the crack troops, who blew up the world's idea of itself and what they once called mankind. Womankind! And a time will come when we can afford to be Women *and* Kind—when it's just and right. Anything else? Yes. Say you've written a book called *Fucking Our Way to Revolution and Socialism*. Some of you probably have for all I know. Say lightly that Michael Foot is a right-wing fascist. It'll get some sort of response, however drowsy. That Chairman Mao is the Kung Fu of gradualism. Talk about going down —with Man—or in any way. You'll find out what 'turns him on'. Cliché but remember you are dealing with men; and men who are the products of a society which turned itself into an almost overnight cliché. Either way, political action always sounds sexy because it means you're violent and passionate even if brainless—so much the better. Yes, you can say things like 'violence is the greatest orgasm of

Historical Experience and Significance'. That'll do for
right *or* left. I'm only talking about the verbal aspects
because it can often save you from the exhausting contortions
of great or famous men. Anything you say about painting
is more or less O.K. As long as it shows you've *heard* of it
and have got reasonable eyesight. Stately homes should be
turned into brothels like mine or abortion clinics; or pads
for squatters, drop-outs and the workers. Whoever they
are it'll amuse you with your perky flight of female mind.
Oh, as for sex, when you get to it: whatever he *wants* if
you can manage it without incurring physical damage. Or
try and talk him into something else. Lots of mouth-work
all round usually works so make sure you haven't had rice
pudding or spinach for lunch. If you wear dentures, you
can even turn it to advantage. While he's luxuriating, toss off
an odd *mot* like 'The Queen should be buggered daily in
the Palace Yard.' If you don't care for the practice yourself
think of something else that isn't entirely repellent to you.
There's always Princess Anne and stallions. Anyone'll
go for that. Just choose the least objectionable lead to the
action. Above all, be spontaneous. That's the only real fun
of it. Do a quick sound out and *play* it. People are best at
it—like women, they're numinously intuitive. Drill into the
ocean bed of your feminine consciousness. Approve or
disapprove. Be disparaging or dismissive. Manically
enthusiastic or just moody and full of hidden hurt and
failure. Men *love* failure. Especially the ones who've made
it early or easy. Or you can be tantalizingly arcane. I have
a lady who always plays records by Wanda Landowska
and talks for ages about her in her midwife's skirt and her
hands poised like gentle hawks over the keyboard. Then
she says 'May I play you some of her Scarlatti?' She
talks about Japs—yes, just about the nastiest race on earth,
so that's imaginative—little dears calling to speckled
deer on their strange flutes. Then she has a record of
Tibetan monks chanting a fifteenth-century prayer to
booming bells. Then it's usually 'Ah, let's go back to
England. To Byrd'. You see she believes—or pretends

to admire and venerate anyone trying to put *significance* into their or our lives. Significance! That's a good stopper. Significance. It's a word that can't even signify. So use it if you like it or it amuses you. It's true—I've miles of her on film doing it. But it is *significant* . . .? To us. It's a ball breaker. 'Now that the captains and the kings have departed.' No, I won't tell you any more about her. She has her own special star quality and she's no chicken either. But what she's done for *us*! Quote unreadable writers like Fanon, Lubin, Marx; be odd but withdrawn about Sylvia Plath; bluff about Ted Hughes. If you really *can't* stand the thought of it all, vomit. Only, take care—he *may* like it. Eat it or something. Men like dirty talk but not about the realities of women's insides so a lot of banter about tubes and afterbirth and tubes and babies' heads and legs and forceps and so on will send some men, especially the nicer ones, really off to the bathroom. . . . Oh, but you will all use your own techniques. Believe me, from what I've seen, the female mind and body is a holy miracle of ingenuity and divine invention. Blake has nothing on HER visions and explorations. That's why we're here. That's *the message*. Right? No questions? . . . On with the final engagement of Life, its very self . . .

(WAIN *enters*.)

WAIN: Mr. Grimthorpe and Mr. Deel are here, m'lady.

REGINE: Send them in. Ladies, we are about to re-enter Paradise. On our own terms. With or without men. Cheers.

(*They all toast. Enter* LEONARD GRIMTHORPE *and* SMASH DEEL. LEONARD *is not bad-looking, fortyish, slightly vague, something of an affection.* SMASH DEEL *is what you'd expect.*) Leonard, how delightful of you to come after all.

LEONARD: Delighted I could make it.

REGINE: And Mr. Deel. Smash—we've all been on edge for hours. Now, let's all get together. There'll be others here soon so we can have a while to get to know one another. You may even know some of us. We have to be careful. You know, ex-wives, people in politics or on newspapers.

LEONARD: I've no worries on any of those scores. But then I'm afraid I take all things as they come. Sorry, cliché first time.

REGINE: Don't worry, darling. We invent them down here. Mr.
Deel, do you know Miss Stella Shrift? Don't worry, she
won't give *you* short shrift though that's her craft and very
good she is at it, I think, don't you?

SMASH: Eh?

REGINE: Now, Leonard, who don't you know?

LEONARD: This lady to begin with.

REGINE: Ah, this is Mrs. Isobel Sands, Leonard Grimthorpe.
Like you, I don't believe she does anything in particular.

LEONARD: Good. Hullo . . .

ISOBEL: Hullo . . .

CURTAIN

END OF ACT ONE

ACT TWO

Scene One

Scene exactly the same but now full with the new arrivals. These are
ROBERT BIGLEY, *a portly young millionaire developer;* STRATFORD
WEST, *the show-biz correspondent referred to in the first Act;*
FREDERICK BLACK, *a rather bored-looking impresario, clearly very
rich;* JOHN STEWKES, *Tory back-bencher, rather like a lofty-looking
suspicious lizard; finally,* ASHLEY WITHERS, *newspaper proprietor, a
jolly, quick, intelligent man, older than most of the others.* REGINE *is
trying to introduce them to the seated and lolling assembly.* SMASH *is
listening to one of his own recordings at the back of the room.*

REGINE: You'll have to sort it out for yourselves. But in no
particular batting order. This is Robert Bigley, the one who
rose from being the son of a self-made—I never understand
what 'self-made' means. We all *make* ourselves. No.
Perhaps you don't agree. Anyway, to become a self-made
millionaire himself. If you want to come here by private
plane or jet to Paris for lunch or helicopter to your box at
the Derby, *all* the Stewards' enclosures of everything,
Henley, Ascot, you name it . . . Founders' Day, Cowes,
he'll be there or get you there quicker and better than anyone.

BIGLEY: I say, Regine, you *are* putting me down and no mistake.

REGINE: You know I admire you irredeemably. I love million-
aires but if they're young it's beyond belief. This is
Stratford West.

WEST: Not to be compared with Stratford East.

REGINE: Darling, you *must* resist that joke. He's always inter-
viewing starlets hot from bosomy film premières. Miss X—
seen in all but the nude. 'Read what *she* says about men
and the older men in particular. She has been a model

39

and played parts in two television series'—yet to be seen.

WEST: That means either they won't be seen or she played a maid or a one-line typist in both.

REGINE: So if you have any theatrical or film ambitions, Stratford's your man. He's also *very* delightful. This is Freddy Black, the impresario. Well, you all know him. Got four hits in the West End. Cases joints like Nottingham, Edinburgh, Bristol, Greenwich, the Royal Court, The Theatre In The Ground, The Theatre On The Roof, like a cat burglar, and transfers them immediately—*if* they get rave notices. Shrewd boy, Freddy. Never backs talent, just a talent for finding backers. Never spent a penny on a production in his life. *Another*, yet another young millionaire! Dear Freddy. The Transfer Dead-Certainty-Only King. *This* is John Stewkes, not a millionaire alas, but brilliant, an M.P., but try to keep off politics because *he* won't. By the way, he's Tory but you needn't worry, he'll disagree with left *and* right. He's sort of left and right of the other circle. Or something like that.

STEWKES: No politics, I promise, Regine. You've just issued an open invitation to your usual insane lefties or your drabbest right-wingers.

REGINE: Don't you think he's a right dandy?

STEWKES: I've been called the smartest man in the House.

REGINE: Goes back to your Oxford Union days, no doubt. Finally, a really powerful figure. Power is so sexy as we all know. Even more than money. I've never had either but I can recognize it, particularly in bed.
(*During this,* LEN *and* ISOBEL *have slipped out.* STELLA *is questioning* WAIN. *He nods towards one of the mirrors.*)

WITHERS: Newspapers don't wield power. They *follow* the news just as they *follow* public taste while they pretend they're leading it. They pinch everything, invent nothing, debase everything. We are the hindsight setters. Lovely to see you, Regine. (*He kisses her.*)

REGINE: Oh, Ashley, you've only just arrived. You've barely touched your second drink.

WITHERS: No point in wasting time.

STELLA: I quite agree. (*To* SMASH, *who is trying to bear hug her out of the room:*) Just a minute, dreamboat. I see that Leonard and Mrs. Sands have anticipated everyone.

REGINE: Well, you know what housewives with no job and teenage children are like. And Leonard's quite a dish, in spite of his awful vagueness.

STELLA: Do you mind? (*She moves to one of the mirrors and looks at it.*)

REGINE: Oh, isn't it a bit early for that?

STELLA: Just this one. For a quick flash off of the first action of the evening.

REGINE: Sorry, if you think it dull, darling.

STELLA: I don't. Really. Please. Does anyone mind?
(*Everyone looks compliant, mutters of approval.* BIGLEY *shouts 'Yahoo' and spills his champagne.*)

REGINE: Wain. The mirror.
(WAIN *presses a button. They all gather around and stare into the mirror. Pause.*)
Good God!

STELLA: They've been in there about forty minutes and they're both sitting on the bed talking like two men in the Athenaeum. Fully clothed.

REGINE: Even got their shoes on. Wain, can we have the sound?

WAIN: Yes, m'lady. (*He presses another switch.*)
(*They all listen in silence. Presently* LEN's *voice can be heard loud and clear.*)

LEONARD (*voice off*): Yes. Yes. That's what I felt. Marriage has to be a commitment *and* poetic. But it's like committed poetry. How can you be committed and really, truly poetic? I mean, it's the poetry that matters. Not the rest of the things in isolation. It's the poetry . . .

ISOBEL: Right. It's that that matters. Then the rest adds up. But if not, no poetry.
(*Pause. They all watch and listen intently. Then:*)

LEONARD (*voice off*): You know . . . do you mind if I talk to you like this?

ISOBEL: No. Anything . . . please . . . it's such a relief.

LEONARD: Well—I—I have considerable difficulty—in getting

41

it up . . .
(*Pause.*)

REGINE: Oh, Christ. Turn it off. It's obscene.

CURTAIN
END OF SCENE ONE

Scene Two

The Bedroom. Furnished as you would expect in this house. ISOBEL *and* LEN *are indeed lying fully clothed on the enormous bed, with about four feet between them. They look cheerful and relaxed, pensive but inquiring and obviously enjoying each other's company. Pause.*)

ISOBEL: Can't you?

LEN: What?

ISOBEL: Get it up?

LEN: Oh, yes. I didn't say I *couldn't* . . . I'm sorry I must have confused you. More champagne?

ISOBEL: Please. . . . Thanks.

LEN: No, it's not that. Only too facile at times. But other times, well. It's about like lifting a mini by hand. Well, not necessarily hand. You know what I mean?

ISOBEL: Exactly. I shouldn't worry about it. You're wonderfully attractive.

LEN: So are you . . . I knew we'd click the minute I saw you.

ISOBEL: So did I.

LEN: Rather conventional, isn't it?

ISOBEL: Very. Do you want me to undress?

LEN: Not just yet. Unless you want to. I think *I* might in a minute. This jacket's frightfully hot and that appalling press of people in Regine's sitting room. Did you like it?

ISOBEL: Not much. I couldn't take my eye off you.

LEN: Well, I was thinking of you . . . I got stuck with that awful journalist woman. Asked me insulting questions and then

42

tried to get me to bring her in here for a quick how's-your-father.

ISOBEL: I thought she'd *got* you for a while.

LEN: Fortunately, Smash Deel started pawing and fumbling at her and I could get away to you. She's probably with him now. She's listed with him, I dare say.

ISOBEL: You mean Lady Frimley has a *placement* for all this?

LEN: Oh, yes. I think we're correctly seated. Just accident though.

ISOBEL: Nice one though.

LEN: Very . . . I say . . .

(*Pause.*)

ISOBEL: What?

LEN: Oh, nothing.

(*Pause.*)

ISOBEL: Wouldn't it be hilarious if we fell in love.

LEN: *That's* what I was going to say. But I funked it . . .

ISOBEL: Did it sound pushy?

LEN: No. Courageous. Are you married?

ISOBEL: Yes.

LEN: Children?

ISOBEL: Three. You?

LEN: Divorced. Three children.

ISOBEL: Snap.

LEN: But you're still married.

ISOBEL: For the present . . .

LEN: Isobel . . . are you religious?

ISOBEL: I don't know. C. of E. But I think, I think it frightens me. Much more than sickness or death.

LEN: Sick unto death. Oh, yes, you're a religious. I could spot you. That's not to say you're not irreverent with yourself. God is in his invisibility. . . . Yes. . . . Odd place to say it. But *think* about it. What we look for is beyond us. We: are: alone in a room. Two strangers. The Jews had a good idea of the heart. I can see yours moving.

ISOBEL: I know. Feel it.

(*He does. Gently.*)

LEN: The Hebrew idea of the heart was—the Whole Man. Not

43

just the intellect. Fools in Christ. We behave like idiots.
That's a bit on the way to heroic. . . . You know what I
said—about not being able to get it up?

ISOBEL: I thought it rather brave . . . I'm afraid *I'm* not very
good at it.

LEN: Aren't you? Neither am I. I don't know . . .
(*They laugh and pour more champagne. Then:*)
What I have, this thing so despised or ignored—is yours.
It sounds strange. We may never? Or never meet again.
But it *would* be yours, not just *my* object. Yours too. *Ours*.
. . . Was that too awful?

ISOBEL: No. Not, not awful. Try not to make me tearful, that's
all.

LEN: Well, that's something we have in common. The Gift of
Tears. Let's cherish that—and drink to it. (*He kisses her
eyes lightly, then her lips.*) You can never be a man, you
know.

ISOBEL: *You* can never be a woman. Isn't it sublime?

LEN: More Shampoo? (*He pours.*) For my *REAL* FRIEND.
(*Another light kiss.*) I don't care, you—women—*are* the
secret of life. *We* are uncertain, undefined, perhaps
unnecessary, as you say. . . . We have to be more:
flamboyant, spurious, enduring, tender, frightened, over-
sensitive and protected, more reckless, indiscreet. You've
been taught that you're a woman of sorts. I that I'm a man.
The Victorians used to, no my father even, thought manli-
ness was an upright virtue. Like thrift. Who recommends
thrift! Nowadays, you can't *consume* and be thrifty. . . .
What was I saying? Girls learn to *be*, boys to *act*. You are a
woman. You are a girl child. You were a virgin. You
became a mother. You *are*. Yet, like me, us, you are still
full of divine discontent.

ISOBEL: I don't think Adam ever *really* lost his rib.

LEN: The effort of learning to live as you're expected to is bad
enough. But to find another way really *is* painful.

ISOBEL: We're none of us sufficiently *prepared*.

LEN: Isobel, I think I love you. I do . . .

ISOBEL: So do I. . . . Is it so strange?

44

LEN: So they'd have us believe. *I* believed it. We've no—
    trouble is—we can't have any clear idea of the future.
ISOBEL: If only it could be an *improved* version of the past.
    With its most particular moments. If it could be open but
    fixed and discernible.
LEN: Pushes white out, drives what in. . . . Have we gone mad?
ISOBEL: No. Neither one of us. Mistaken perhaps but that's
    not madness.
LEN: We can never *know* each other. Do you think you can be
    unsexed by failure?
ISOBEL: No . . . more likely success, like those rich young men in
    Regine's room.
LEN: All-exacting affairs, all-exacting marriages. No middle
    ground unless it's just doggerel. You get pretty sick of
    doggerel.
ISOBEL: It's the poetry *we're* after.
LEN: You're dead right. It's the poetry we're after. That's the
    middle bit we're after! Didn't you say that earlier sometime?
ISOBEL: No. *You* did.
    (LEONARD *starts to undress in a rather baffled way, not yet
    drunk but slightly confused by his encounter with* ISOBEL.)
LEN: Funny, meeting *you* here.
ISOBEL: Yes.
LEN: Sorry. Lot. Who said Art is made by the alone for the
    alone?
ISOBEL: Don't know. (*She watches him carefully undressing.*)
    Sounds true.
LEN: Do you? Yes. So do I. That's why we need Love.
    Otherwise we *would* be alone. Frighteningly. There's not
    that much Art. . . . Doesn't bear thinking about . . .
ISOBEL: Don't fret.
LEN: Sorry. Dirty habit. In public, anyway.
ISOBEL: I wonder what the others are doing.
LEN: Don't care, do you?
ISOBEL: No. I've got—no, she's, Wain's put in some Shampoo
    for real friends.
    (*He kisses her. He is now without jacket or trousers. He goes
    to a concealed built-in fridge and opens another bottle. They*

toast each other after the silence.)

LEN: To real friends.

ISOBEL: Real friends. Shampoo. Are we being rude to our hostess? Disappearing so soon?

LEN: Hell no. That's what we're here for. Well, not us so much. We're more or less nobodies. A whim of Regine's. The whole joint is bugged like Watergate. Two-way mirrors. God knows what.

(ISOBEL *looks slightly alarmed.*)

Don't mind, do you?

ISOBEL: I don't know. They must be pretty busy themselves by this time. Miss Shrift and Smash!

LEN: Shall I turn the light off?

ISOBEL: No, please . . .

LEN: You've nothing to worry about. You look heart-bearing.

ISOBEL: Thanks. . . . So do you . . .

(*Looks down at himself.*)

LEN: Do I? Really? My wife used to say no man could look sexy in his socks.

ISOBEL: Your wife was wrong.

LEN: But right for *her*. But not for you.

ISOBEL: No.

LEN: Anyway, if you don't mind, I think I'll take them off. I've got disgusting feet, I'm afraid.

ISOBEL: Go ahead . . .

LEN: I can't believe it.

ISOBEL: What?

LEN: About you being no good at it.

ISOBEL: I've been *told*.

LEN: Don't believe interested parties—if that's what I mean. . . . Yes, it is.

ISOBEL: I think they were right.

LEN: Well, it all—all—

ISOBEL: Yes?

LEN: Depends on what—I mean who it is. Surely? No?

ISOBEL: Perhaps. But there must be a minimum standard of performance.

LEN: Yes. Like my not getting it up. Good model but difficult

46

to start. Use plenty of choke.

ISOBEL: To at least give pleasure. If not *please*.

LEN: You know that's what's nice about women. They don't
mind your beer belly or your bad breath or—bad breath . . .

ISOBEL: Your grey hair. That's nice.

LEN: Ageing.

ISOBEL: You're young. That's what's nice about men. They can
still be boys and yet men. Women can't do that trick.

LEN: Not so retarded.

ISOBEL: People think I'm arrogant. They don't know the *effort*
it takes . . . I'm . . . tired of effort . . .

LEN: My dear. (*Solicitously.*) Take your shoes off . . . (*He takes
them off and rubs her feet.*) Better?

ISOBEL: Not bad for a man with your physical disadvantages . . .

LEN: My children don't care too much for me. What about yours?

ISOBEL: They make excuses for me.

LEN: I spent months alone in an Anderson air-raid shelter
during the war. What with that and school, by the time I
was sixteen I was heartily sick of myself.

ISOBEL: Life may be hell but who can tell that unknown boredom
from which no traveller returns.

LEN: Perhaps we're reincarnated.
(*During the rest of the scene, they are both slowly undressing.
He unzips her at one point. As they chat.*)

ISOBEL: Do you remember *Margaret Rose*?

LEN: *Rather!* Have you ever thought of a woman er, well:
fishing—alone; bird-watching alone; being a game-keeper;
lighthouse keeper; butterfly collector?
(*Pause.*)

ISOBEL: No.

LEN: Neither can I. I can't imagine myself either. I'd like to see
you, oh, say, bird-watching.

ISOBEL: Ambition . . . Amazonian.

LEN: *Travel* agents! Ugh!

ISOBEL: Can you imagine anyone painting their friends?

LEN: I suppose they do.

ISOBEL: Yes, but how many? Can you think of a woman as a
comrade? Not a thick communist, you understand?

47

LEN: Yes. . . . Yes. I can. Who will be tomorrow's *portraits*?

ISOBEL: Do you think woman can connect? Like priests say.

LEN: Difficult that one. Yes. I do. But by their insides. Nuns
are pretty funny. Just think of a world where masturbation
is TAUGHT. To the WANKING classes of the world—
unite! *You* may not be able to get it up sometime.

ISOBEL: 'Whereof one cannot speak,
Thereof one must be silent.'

LEN: I mean a chap must be utterly chaotic inside?

ISOBEL: How else to give birth to a dancing star?

LEN: Dreading pain. Paining Dread.

(*By this point, they are both* almost *totally unclothed. They
slide into bed almost absent-mindedly like a long-married
couple and sit up talking in the same manner as before.*)
Where is the fall of the sparrow now? Where's the bloody
sparrow?

ISOBEL: I think *we* might be a couple of sparrows.

LEN: So do I, you know. (*Hums.*)
'Singing like a sparrow on the top of a tree.' There is she.

ISOBEL: There is he. Waving of their handkerchees.

LEN: ⎫ (*Together.*) 'Singing like two sparrows on the top of a
ISOBEL: ⎭ tree!'

(*They giggle slightly.*)

LEN: Fancy you knowing that!

ISOBEL: Fancy *you* knowing it. Bit before both our times.

LEN: Music hall. *You* liked that.

ISOBEL: Some women actually enjoy jokes too, you know.

LEN: I suppose they must do. It's *our* fault. We oversell them.
And get all loud and noisy and hectoring.

ISOBEL: My son says he's going to be a drop-out.

LEN: The trouble with that is someone may not pick you up
but just leave you there.

ISOBEL: Exactly what I told him.

LEN: You may be a falling or fallen star. But you can't be a
prone one. Not for starters, anyway . . .

ISOBEL: People ask me if I worry about him. . . . Don't you hate
those people who say: *Will it be all right?*

LEN: The Doomsters. How will you manage. Aren't you *worried*?

48

But supposing that . . .? Isn't it a bit of a risk? Yes, it
bloody well *is*! I was at risk the moment I drew breath.
I'll bet the Wright Brothers had some cheery neighbours.
Supposing it just falls down, Orville? Aren't you *worried*,
Mr. Galileo? But do you think the *Pope* will like it,
Michaelangelo? Sure you don't want to change your mind,
J.C? You look awfully *uncomfortable* up there. But it's only
an ordinary little *apple*, Sir Isaac. My wife has silly dreams
all the time, Dr. Freud. We're *always laughing* at them.

ISOBEL: You know the one about the professor who'd heard that
there was still a very old attendant at the British Museum
who remembered Karl Marx going into the Reading Room?

LEN: No?

ISOBEL: Well, the visiting professor finally tracks down this
ancient old attendant and asks him if he remembers Karl
Marx in the Reading Room. Mr. Marx? says the old man.
Mr. Marx? Oh yes, I remember him very well. Bearded
gentleman. Used to come in every day for years. Could
set your watch by him. Every day for years. Every day
for years. Then, one day, he didn't turn up and—and he
never came in again! Never. Funny thing. *And nobody's
heard anything of him ever since!*

LEN: Don't you worry about your eyesight, Mr. Marx? The
thing is to use *your* language and not someone else's.

ISOBEL: Exactly. I seem to have been mouthing other people's
words all these years . . . Not my own.

LEN: But—well, like in marriage, no, not just marriage: how
does one avoid cruelty? And still be honest and *survive*?
Do you like nudes? Female, of course. Male doesn't
count. It's only fit for photography.

ISOBEL: Yes. I do. It's the eternal subject.

LEN: Glorious pursuit of the *impossible*. All nude painting is
religious. It's exploring the unknowable.

ISOBEL: Like God.

LEN: Distorted bodies, ravaged bodies, sad bodies, proud
bodies. All *points* in the great circle . . . I'm so glad.

ISOBEL: Thanks.

LEN: The trouble with my wife was that I *confided* in her. Too much. Too rich for the blood. And it would come back at me later like a brick. No. That was a mistake. Confiding. Overdid it. Not enough restraint. Do you have restraint?

ISOBEL: I ape it. But that's all.

LEN: I once knew a couple—both divorced—who married each other because the *children* wanted them to!

ISOBEL: People like that give heterosexuals a bad name.

LEN: It's the food of all painters and their nudes, the priests with their clouds of unknowing. Marriage should be a vision of excellence. EXCELLENCE. The stuff they don't make or want any more.

ISOBEL: No demand for it nowadays, madam.

LEN: But a *vision*.

ISOBEL: A vision.

(*They turn to look at each other. Pause.*)

LEN: I *am* in love with you. (*Puzzled pleasure.*)

ISOBEL: And I with you . . .

LEN: Isn't it extraordinary . . .?

ISOBEL: Weird . . .

LEN: Shall we?

ISOBEL: Yes . . .

(*They embrace.*)

LEN: Shall I turn the light out?

ISOBEL: No . . .

LEN: Remember——

ISOBEL: Yes?

LEN: Well, if I . . . No, it's going to be all right.

ISOBEL: It will. Desire shall not fail. . . . And you remember . . .

LEN: What?

ISOBEL: It's only a vision.

LEN: And that's what we're both after.

ISOBEL: A vision . . .

(*They embrace.*)

CURTAIN

END OF SCENE TWO

Scene Three

The Sitting Room. Early morning. ISOBEL *is lying on a sofa with* LEN's *head in her lap. They are both fully dressed, very sleepy and contented almost to the point of smugness.* WAIN *comes in with a breakfast tray and sets it down before them. He coughs.*

ISOBEL: Oh, thank you, Wain. I'm starving.

LEN: So am I.

ISOBEL: After all that exercise. Talk about Olympic Games.

LEN: Well, you're certainly the Muhammad Ali of the century.
    You *are* the greatest, man.

ISOBEL: And you're the greatest, man.
    (*They kiss.*)

LEN: Not very good at it! You're the World Cup winner.

ISOBEL: Can't get it up! Down more likely. *Down*, Fido!

LEN: Well, Fido is a bit sore this morning, I must admit.

ISOBEL: I'm surprised he's still *there*. What about *me*! *My* vision's
    pretty sore round its edges.

LEN: Darling. You *are* a vision.

ISOBEL: So are you. Let's eat before we slope off.
    (REGINE *enters*.)

REGINE: Oh, good morning, you two. Up already. Sleep well?

ISOBEL: Not a wink.

LEN: Not one.

ISOBEL: Marvellous.

LEN: Magnificent.

ISOBEL: Super, comfy bed, Regine.

REGINE: Well, I'm glad it was such a success. You both look as
    if you've had a—vision.

ISOBEL: We have.

LEN: The two of us.

ISOBEL: A flash only——

LEN: But such a flash . . .

ISOBEL: Of the journey.

LEN: We don't know where we're going.

ISOBEL: And we never shall.

LEN: But we've *started* the journey.

ISOBEL: Together.

LEN: Like Paul and Barnabas.

ISOBEL: Perhaps we should re-name ourselves.

LEN: You be Paul——

ISOBEL: And you be Barnabas.

LEN: Morning, Paul.

ISOBEL: Howdy, Barnabas.

    (*They kiss.*)

LEN: Had any good visions lately?

ISOBEL: Ecstatic.

LEN: So have I.

ISOBEL: But I'm a bit new to this missioning and journeys.

LEN: Me too. But we'll pick it up.

ISOBEL: We *have* picked it up.

REGINE: You two are very odd. Don't tell me you've——

ISOBEL: Fallen in love?

LEN: Utterly.

REGINE: You *are* mad. Perhaps the country air doesn't agree
    with you. That champagne was all right, wasn't it, Wain?

WAIN: Yes, m'lady.

REGINE: Have all the others breakfasted?

WAIN: They're all down.

REGINE: Good.

WAIN: Or gone.

REGINE: Gone? Who?

WAIN: The gentlemen, m'lady.

REGINE: But who? Why?

WAIN: Mr. Nates and Mr. Bigley left in Mr. Bigley's helicopter.
    They said to say: Thanks for all the *wild* entertainment.
    And they'd 'see you around'. Mr. West said he'd not
    enjoyed himself so much for years. He'd ring you from
    Fleet Street. He went back to 'file some copy' in his office.
    Mr. Black had to go to a preview in the provinces some-
    where. He said to thank you for all the fun and he'd be

getting to you about backing his new show. Mr. Stewkes
apologized but said he had to go to his constituency
surgery and also prepare a speech for the House next week
about blackmail and vice in the country. Mr. Deel's group
arrived in a van to take him to a gig in Newcastle. He told
me to tell you he'd had a great, funky time. Mr. Withers
left in his car. He said he had to 'get to the bank as soon
as it opened'. He told me to *tell* you. Mr. Stan had given
him a letter of authorization.

REGINE: Letter of authorization! My God, they'll have opened it
already.

WAIN: He asked me to give you this note.

(*She tears it open and reads it aloud.*)

REGINE: 'National Newspapers Ltd. Male is gender—chauvinist
is excessive love of country. Pigs is ladies' jargon. I know
you've been "had" many times but not like this. Thank
you for a delightful and enjoyable stay in your gorgeous
place. Kindest wishes for now and the future, yours gratefully
and patriotically, Ashley Withers.'
The snake!!

LEN: Not pigs.

ISOBEL: I *like* piggies.

REGINE: Get Mr. Stan, will you.

WAIN: He's putting his suitcases in the car, m'lady.

REGINE: Suitcases! Everyone's gone mad! Get him in here.

(WAIN *goes out.*

STELLA, LETITIA, JOG *and* GWEN *enter.*)

STELLA: *I'm* mad with that Smash Deel. My wrist is falling off.
How were yours?

LETITIA: So-so. Usual.

GWEN: Draggy.

JOG: Real PIGGY. Horrible. Men! They won't know what's
hit them.

STELLA: Those two look very starry.

REGINE: *They're* in love, my dear.

FOUR GIRLS: In love!

STELLA: Is there a doctor in the house!

LETITIA: What larks!

53

GWEN: But is he filthy rich or something?

JOG: Just *filthy*! Ugh!

REGINE: Everything's gone wrong. There's been a plot to bring us down.

JOG: Counter-revolutionary?

REGINE: You bet your life it's counter-revolutionary. And my Stan, my STAN has been the one under the counter right from the outset.

STELLA: Stan. But he's a, a NO-man.

REGINE: He's a man all right. Treacherous. Betrayer. (*Calls*) Stan! Stan! *Judas!*

(STAN *comes in armed with camera equipment and a plane ticket in his hand.*)

STAN: Call me?

REGINE: Where do you think you're going?

STAN: Sunny Spain.

STELLA: On holiday?

STAN: No. To live. For good. Nice and luxurious. Own villa, birds, everything.

REGINE: To *live*! What about *us*?

STAN: You've got this, haven't you? Anyhow, we're not married or anything like that.

REGINE: Where's last night's film and photographs and everything?

STAN: Gave them to the newspaper proprietor geezer. Withers.

REGINE: You *gave* it to him! (*It really is sinking into her now.*) And the rest! All the archives! The boxes! The bank!

STAN: Oh, he's got the lot.

REGINE: *All* of it!

STAN: All of it. He just rang me to say he'd got it safely. I'm picking up my cheque on the way to the airport.

REGINE: Cheque!

STAN: How else do you think I can live in Spain for the rest of my life and never lift a finger?

STELLA: You little *rat*!

LETITIA: Traitor!

GWEN: Scum!

JOG: Fascist!

54

STAN: Well, I'll be off then. 'Bye, ladies. Nice seeing you.

ISOBEL: Good night, ladies. Sweet ladies . . .

LEN: Good night, good night, good night.

JOG: You won't get away with this! We'll start the fight all over again. *All* revolutions have their setbacks and traitors.

STELLA: My God. All over again!

REGINE: All that work and preparation. It'll take *years*.

JOG: Don't fail now, comrades! This will make us *stronger*, not *weaker*.

LEN: It's like the Lisbon earthquake. You can interpret its meaning to suit your OWN prejudice.

JOG: Shut up, you *beast*!

LEN: To RAIL is the privilege of the loser. Anyway, men's sins are mostly VENIAL rather than venereal, as *you* appear to believe.

JOG: We *hate* you, all of you. *Hate* you.

LEN: In the case of you ladies, perfect hatred understandeth all things.

ISOBEL: And perfect hatred casteth out all fear.

STELLA: What are you: a double act?

STAN: Well, I'm off then. Don't try to do anything *I* can.

REGINE: Good riddance!

ALL FOUR: Pig!

STAN: Well, honk honk and tickerty boo! (*He leaves.*)
(JOG *is almost having a fit.*)

JOG: Go! Our time is *coming*. It's coming, comrades, when we *shall* say: (*She stands on a sofa. And declares*)
'O, withered is the garland of the war;
The soldier's pole is fall'n
Young boys and girls are level now with men!'
(ISOBEL *gets up on another sofa.*)

ISOBEL: And do you know how that goes on?
'The odds is gone.
And there is nothing left remarkable
Beneath the visiting moon.'

JOG: Renegade bitch! Sex traitor!

LEN: I think it's time we left, darling. *We're* a minority group.
(*He helps her down. To* REGINE:) Thank you for the most

divine weekend I've ever had.

ISOBEL: Divine!

(*They go hand in hand up centre to the door.*)

LEN: And always remember, ladies. At least in *your* cases:
'A WOMAN IS A WOMAN BUT A GOOD CIGAR
IS A *SMOKE*!'

CURTAIN

THE END

Jill and Jack
a play for television

CAST

JILL

JACK

MARY

MARK

WILFRED

JERRY

WILLIE

GUARD

PORTER

MILLS

WAITER

CLUB MEMBER

CABBIE

GIRL ON TRAIN

WOMAN ON TRAIN

POLICEMAN

Jill and Jack was first transmitted by Yorkshire Television on 11th September 1974 when the cast was as follows:

WILFRED	Stanley Lebor
JILL	Jill Bennett
JERRY	Denis Lawson
MARY	Wendy Gifford
JACK	John Standing
MARK	Michael Byrne
GIRL ON TRAIN	Alison Mead
WAITER	Alan Bowlas

Directed by Mike Newell
Produced by Peter Willes

1. EXT. NIGHT

A discreet but expensive car turns off a busy London street and makes its smooth, chauffeur-driven way into the leafy space of an attractive square. It stops outside one of the tall early nineteenth-century houses. The uniformed chauffeur emerges to open the door for JILL *who steps out unhurriedly from reading her paper from the lamp in the roomy comfort of the back. She is attractive and dressed in the most strikingly stylish but succinctly everyday way.*

WILFRED: Your brief-case, madam.
(*He hands it to her and she takes it, folding her paper carefully but naturally.*)
JILL: Thank you, Wilfred. How long do we need to get there?
WILFRED: Oh, twenty minutes should be about right in this traffic.
JILL: Right. I'll be out in fifteen. Just in case there are any hold-ups on the way.
WILFRED: Very good, madam.
JILL: Don't want to keep him waiting. You know how they worry.
WILFRED: That's right, madam.
(*She goes up the steps to the front door, which is opened by* JERRY, *a young man in a smart white jacket.*)
JERRY: Good evening, madam.

2. INT. ENTRANCE HALL NIGHT

JILL: Evening, Jerry. Put my brief-case in the study on my desk, will you.

JERRY: Yes, madam.

JILL: Only I may have to go over a few things later—if I
get the chance.

JERRY: Your evening papers, madam.

JILL: Thanks.

(*Takes them.*)

Only I've got to dash.

(*Unhurried, she glances at papers.*)

JERRY: Hectic day, madam?

JILL: Just the usual, Jerry. Just the usual. Frantic but
fun. . . . Fun but frantic. I could do with a drink
while I'm changing.

(*She advances towards the stairs, taking in the headlines and
stop press.*)

JERRY: I put some of the Chablis on ice in your room.

JILL: Thanks. Miss Kaye in?

JERRY: In her room. I think she's taking someone to the
theatre.

JILL (*to self*): That self-loving squirt Robert, I suppose.

(*She goes upstairs.*)

JERRY: You are *both* dining out tonight?

JILL: Yes. I shall be at my club. But there shouldn't be
anything. So you might as well go out for the
evening.

JERRY: That's very nice, madam. I'll leave everything out you
might need when you come in.

JILL: Thanks.

3. INT.   UPSTAIRS CORRIDOR   NIGHT

Following JILL, *past good paintings, furnishings, etc., into:*

4. INT.   JILL'S BEDROOM   NIGHT

*It is large, with a double bed and all sorts of dizzy consumer
luxuries like hi-fi, fridges, etc., leading on to her own leafy, exotic
bathroom and dressing-room. A parrot swings in the bathroom,
highly coloured, cheerful, called* WILLIE. *She turns on some music*

and starts to undress methodically and without particular hurry.
Clearly, she has the operation timed to a second. Still glancing
at the headlines and back pages for the racing results, she goes to
her large wardrobe.

JILL: Damn.

WILLIE: Damn!

JILL: Evening, Willie. That horse was nowhere. You gave
    me the wrong tip.

WILLIE: Nowhere! Nowhere! Damn!

JILL: I wish you'd draw me a bath and shut up, you dozy,
    past-it old pullet.

(She makes a quick selection from an almost endless line of
dresses and shoes and places them on the bed carefully.)

5. INT. BATHROOM NIGHT

JILL: Nothing to wear, as usual.

WILLIE: Past-it old pullet.

JILL: *You* are, not me!

(She draws the bath, goes back and pours herself some wine
from the waiting bucket. She carefully selects stockings from
a drawer as she buzzes the house phone.)

JILL (*on phone*): Jerry! I've just tried the wine. It can't be
    the usual . . . no, I know it wasn't. Chateau Y-Front
    '69 I'd say. Send it back, will you. Can't think *what*
    they're doing. Right . . .

(As she puts down the receiver, there is a knock on the door.)

JILL: Mary? Come in.

(MARY enters, dressed for a big evening.)

MARY: Hullo! Rush?

JILL: No. I've six minutes or so. You?

MARY: Well, you know Robert. He'll only fret if I'm not
    there first.

JILL: How would he *know*?

MARY: He'd just *know*, that's all. Right?

JILL: I *do* know, thanks.

MARY: Shagged?

63

JILL: Drink'll put me right. That bloody horse didn't come in.

MARY: Not anywhere?

WILLIE: Not anywhere!

JILL: Willie—shut up. I'll cut off your beak at *both* ends. (*All very light, by the way. Like the rest, in fact.*)

JILL: Where you off to then? Not that bloody Crush Bar again?

MARY: He likes it. Got to keep 'em happy.

JILL: Suppose so.

MARY: And it's Nureyev or something and he likes to be *seen*. Yes. SEEN! You know how they like to be *seen*.

JILL: That's all they go for as far as I can make out.

MARY: And you?

JILL: Just the club.

MARY: Bit dull for him, isn't it?

JILL: He doesn't seem to mind. As long as he's with me.

MARY: Lucky old you.

JILL: There's my bath.

WILLIE: Bath's nowhere!

(JILL *goes over to the bathroom.*)

MARY: You'll be late.

JILL: *You* will. And you know what *that'll* do to the evening.

MARY: Don't I just! Two ten quid tickets for nowt. See you.

JILL: No oats if you don't *run* for 'em! 'Bye.

MARY: Have fun!

JILL: Oh, I think I shall . . .

(*She watches* MARY *go out. As she turns into the bathroom for her bathing cap,* WILLIE *shouts past.*)

WILLIE: Have fun! Nowhere! Have fun. Have fun.

6. INT. JACK'S FLAT NIGHT

In the inner suburbs which he shares with MARK. *Perhaps, at this point it should be made absolutely clear that neither* JACK *nor* MARK *are remotely 'Gay' to use the fashionable cant word. The same applies to* JILL *and* MARY. *They are very much two chaps and two girls. It is merely that their social roles have become rather confused, if not completely reversed.* JACK *is sweating in front of the mirror trying to fix his bow tie before putting the finishing touches to his evening outfit.*

JACK: Oh, great balls of bleeding fire. Why did I have to put on a new shirt. Sackfuls of plastic knicker elastic and pins and cardboard. Damn plastic.

MARK (*appears round door*): And down with elastic. Can I help?

JACK: Why can't I buy a decent shirt! Instead of this floppy dicky's night out!

MARK: Car's here.

JACK: Tell him he can wait.

MARK: Train won't.

JACK: Could you give us a hand?

MARK: Easy as winking. Don't panic. You want to look your best. All that. That's what they want . . .

(*He helps tie-making.*)

JACK: 'Course it is. Then when we look like a bundle of old rags. . . . Bless you, old boy. You are good at these things.

MARK: Have to be, old darling. Don't we all? There we are!

JACK: May the Good Lord bless you and all that. I could kiss you. In fact I will.

(*He does, perfunctorily.*)

Hand me my jacket, will you?

MARK: *Very* nice! Present?

JACK: Her.

MARK: Thought so. Bang-on taste.

JACK (*anxious*): I say, old boy, you don't think——

MARK: You look——

JACK: The waistcoat's a bit——

MARK: What?

JACK: Well . . . poncified.

MARK: She'll adore it. And the watch and chain.

JACK: Really?

MARK: Really.

JACK: You're not just saying that. She's so meticulous
    herself. I'd hate her to think . . .
MARK: Think?
JACK: Well, that I'm all done up like a dog's dinner just
    because I want her to, well, you know.
MARK: Rubbish. She'll be thrilled with you. So she should
    be. Some girls'd go potty. What's that?
JACK: What's what!
MARK: Scent?
JACK: Oh, God—do I smell? I did my armpits. My socks
    gleaming like confetti. Pure, fresh. *Do* I look an ass?
MARK: No. Irresistible.
JACK: You don't think I should put on the old trusty green
    and brown——
MARK: Pinstripe. No. I don't.
(*Horn honks outside.*)
    Now get your skates on. You know how it irritates
    them if you're a few minutes late.
JACK: Thanks, dear heart. You've been a brick.
(*He dashes to the door.*)
MARK: Have a nice evening. Relax. She'll adore you.
JACK: Oh, I hope so. Oh, oh, my overnight case.
MARK: Do you think you should?
JACK: Well, we'll see. Depends how she—er—puts it.
MARK: She knows how to behave. Well, I'll see you. Or not.
JACK: Yes. Or not.
(*Horn off.*)
MARK: Go on!
JACK: Yes. Great night. Big deal. I'll never get through it.
    Oh, my gawd!

7.   EXT. HOUSE NIGHT

He stumbles down the steps outside and falls into the waiting cab.

MARK (*calling out*): Bonne chance!
JACK: Thanks, old boy. Bless you.
CABBIE: Well?

JACK: Station!

8. EXT. RAILWAY STATION NIGHT

JACK *dashes through the barrier, past the ticket inspector and is assisted on to the moving train by a porter.*

9. INT. CROWDED RAILWAY CARRIAGE NIGHT

JACK *is looking rather flushed and uneasy, as he stands, clutching his overnight case. A* YOUNG GIRL *looks up at him curiously from her seat.*

YOUNG GIRL: Excuse me, but are you feeling all right?
JACK: Yes, thank you.
YOUNG GIRL (*starting to rise*): You look to me as if you'd be better sitting down.
JACK: No, really, thank you. I think I need a bit of fresh air.
YOUNG GIRL: Very well. If you're sure.
(*She goes back to reading her paper and he gropes his way through the door to the corridor.*)

10. INT. RAILWAY CORRIDOR NIGHT

JACK *stumbles his way past bad-tempered passengers to the lavatory. It is marked 'engaged'. He waits and presently a man and a woman emerge. He turns cheerfully to a man who has to stand back.*

JACK: Well, perhaps they *are* engaged!
(*He goes in.*)

11. INT. RAILWAY TRAIN LAVATORY NIGHT

JACK *tidies himself up, hair, collar, tie, waistcoat, etc. Presently, a woman's voice is heard as there is a banging on the door.*

WOMAN (*V.O.*): How much longer are you going to be!
JACK: Oh, bloody shut up. Impatient bitch.
(*He goes through his bag, taking out pyjamas, shaving kit and so on.*)
      Two packets. Well: I'll be leaving all that to her.
(*He opens the window and throws something out. Then emerges from the lavatory, all 'tidied up' to meet a very angry looking girl. He smiles at her sweetly.*)
      All yours.

12. EXT. PLATFORM LONDON RAILWAY TERMINAL NIGHT

JACK *gets down gingerly—No, not gingerly, but careful of his appearance and looks around expectantly. Disappointed at seeing no-one, he goes to the barrier but can't find his ticket.*

JACK: Well, it's here somewhere. I'm not trying to get a
     free ride. Like some of *you* lot.
(*The* GUARD *almost yawns in his face as he waits for the elusive ticket.*)

13. EXT. OUTSIDE TERMINAL CONCOURSE NIGHT

JILL *is waiting in the car with* WILFRED *in front. She looks at her watch. A* POLICEMAN *approaches.*

POLICEMAN: Not allowed to park here. See up there.
JILL: Won't be a moment, constable.
(*She leans forward to* WILFRED.)
     You go round for a bit or find a space or something
    and I'll go and see if I can find him. Probably lost
    his ticket or dropped his case.

14. EXT. STATION NIGHT

She gets out and crosses to the main hall. Indeed, JACK *is picking*

68

up his toiletry, which has dropped out of his case. She goes over to him.

JILL: Jack.
JACK: Darling!
(*They embrace fiercely. Then:*)
JILL: I suppose we'd better pick this lot up.
(*She bends down as* JACK *re-adjusts himself to the situation.*)

15. INT. CAR NIGHT

JILL *and* JACK *in the back while* WILFRED *drives.*

JILL: Darling, you look stunning.
JACK: Do you think so? I feel a wreck.
JILL: Well, you aren't. You're fabulous.
JACK: I can't do. Not after that journey.
JILL: You must believe me, sometimes.
JACK: Well, Mark helped.
JILL: How is he?
JACK: O.K. I suppose I was hoping you'd be on the plat-
    form, waiting . . .
JILL: Well, I thought we'd get away quicker. This way.
    Parking and all . . .
JACK (*absently*): Oh, yes. . . . Where are we going?
JILL: I thought we'd go to the club. If you don't mind.
JACK: Sounds fine. Am I allowed in?
JILL: Thursday dinner and Sunday lunch. Some of the
    older members fought a desperate rearguard action to
    keep you out altogether but I'm afraid even they had
    to move with the times. Progress?
JACK (*uninterested*): Ah, yes.
JILL: Actually, you're my first gentleman guest.
JACK: As long as I'm with you. I don't care where.
(*They clasp hands.*)
JILL: I hope it won't be too stuffy. For you, I mean. But
    it *is* a special sort of occasion.
JACK: Oh, good. I love special occasions.

EXT. NIGHT

Neoclassical exterior of JILL's *club. The car draws up.*

JACK: Damn! It's raining.

JILL: Never mind.

JACK: I *do* mind. I only went to the crimpers this afternoon.

JILL: Wilfred's got the umbrella, haven't you, Wilfred?

JACK: Especially. Cost me two quid. It's *pouring*! What about my jacket? Mark pressed it for me particularly.

JILL: It'll be all right.

JACK: I can't do these things myself . . . all right!

(*He snorts at the rain and churlishly lets himself be escorted out of the car under the cover of* WILFRED's *umbrella.* JILL *follows him, uncovered in the rain. In the entrance to the club,* JACK *shakes himself like a frenzied dog.*)

JILL: There! Wasn't much. All right?

JACK (*glaring*): What do *you* think?

(JILL *bites her lip slightly and turns to* WILFRED.)

JILL: Put the car in the corner garage, will you, Wilfred? I'll drive us home.

WILFRED: Very good, madam.

JACK: Are we going to stay out here all night? I'm bloody freezing.

JILL: You and I have got an early start in the morning.

WILFRED: Yes, madam.

JACK: Oh, *do* come on!

JILL: Coming, darling.

WILFRED: Good night, madam.

JILL: Good night, Wilfred. Have a nice evening.

WILFRED: Thank you. Very kind of you. Good night, sir.

JACK: Oh!!

(*He blunders bearishly through the glass doors, assisted by* WILFRED. JILL *follows.*)

17. INT. CLUB NIGHT

Vast spiral staircase. Like the Reform or Travellers', etc. JILL *nods genially to the* CLUB PORTER *in his glass fortress, who responds with nice respect.* JACK *is still brushing himself down.*

JACK: My shirt looks a right old mess.
JILL: Don't fret. Honestly, darling——
JACK: Would you show me to the Men's—if you've got one in this place.
JILL: Certainly. (*To the* PORTER:) Would you show my guest to the Gentlemen's cloakroom?
(PORTER *nods and leads* JACK *up the first bank of stairs to the right.*)
JACK: I can't possibly go in like this.
JILL: Take your time, darling. I'll have a drink ready for you.
JACK: Oh—aren't you going to wait for me, then?
JILL: I'll be in the bar. You know how long you take. The porter will show you.
JACK: Oh, all right then.
(*He disappears with the* PORTER.)

18. INT. CLUB NIGHT

JILL *proceeds on her way up the great staircase. She nods to one or two other lady members. All over the walls are portraits of women in Judges' wigs, academic gowns and so on. Upstairs she settles into a huge leather armchair. A* CLUB SERVANT *approaches.*

SERVANT: Good evening, madam.
JILL: Evening, Mills.
MILLS: Usual?
JILL: Please, Mills. For two. Ah!
(*Her face, which has been slightly strained, lightens as a fellow member approaches her.*)

19. INT. CLUB NIGHT

JACK *enters the room, uneasy in the unfamiliar surroundings and still slightly petulant. The other member drifts off.*

71

JILL: Over here, darling. Drink's all ready.

JACK (*sits*): Oh, there you are.

JILL: Your favourite. All right now?

JACK: Just about.

JILL: That's good then. Cheers.

JACK: Cheers. Sorry to keep you waiting.

JILL: Couldn't matter less. We've all evening.

JACK: Yes. You seemed to be enjoying yourself with your
    friend. Who's she then?

JILL: Just another member. Nice, lively girl. Very bright.

JACK: I'm sure. Business, I suppose. Talk, talk, talk . . .

JILL: We don't discuss business here.

JACK: Oh, what do you *discuss* then?

JILL: We come for, oh, the usual, companionship, convivi-
    ality. To enjoy ourselves. Which is what we're going to
    do tonight.

JACK: Yes . . .

JILL: I've ordered a smashing dinner. Your favourite
    asparagus and—oh, you'll see.
    (*Pause.*) Drink O.K.?

JACK: Fine.

JILL: I think they make the best in London.

JACK: Yes?

JILL: Yes. . . . What do *you* think?

JACK: Wouldn't know.

JILL: Well, cheers, my darling.

JACK: What?

JILL: To us.

JACK: Oh, yes.

(*He raises his glass. Pause.*)

JILL: Comfortable in that chair?

JACK: My shirt's still damp.

JILL: I'm sorry.

JACK: Oh, does it show?

JILL: No. Not at all.

JACK: Where?

JILL: Not anywhere. Really.

(*Pause.*)

72

JACK: Have I done anything wrong?

JILL: Wrong? Why?

JACK: Oh, I don't know. A bit——

JILL: What?

JACK: Oh, nothing. I'll only put my foot in it.

JILL: A bit what am I?

JACK: Oh—funny, that's all.

JILL: In what way 'funny'?

JACK: Oh, forget it. Maybe it's me as usual.

JILL: You?

JACK: You are pleased to see me, aren't you?

JILL: I've been looking forward to it all day. I couldn't think of anything else.

JACK: Is everything all right?

JILL: Why shouldn't it be?

JACK: Don't shout at me.

JILL: I'm *not*!

JACK: It's just that I get these funny feelings.

JILL: We're together, that's all that matters.

JACK: Insecure. I know it's a bore to someone like you.

JILL: Darling, you're never a bore to me.

JACK: You mean I am to others.

JILL: *No*body thinks you're a bore. Least of all me. I adore you . . .

JACK: Oh, well, sorry.

JILL: Darling . . . relax. . . . Hungry?

JACK: Gone off it a bit. All that bloody rain. I don't mean to moan.

JILL: You're not moaning. Anyway, why shouldn't you have a good old moan? Tell me. I've had quite a day myself.

JACK: Oh, well, of course, it's nothing like you——

JILL: Now, come on——

JACK: Only I did want to see you so much and be at my best.

JILL: Yes?

JACK: And everything seemed to go wrong.

JILL: I know. But that's done with.

JACK: I sup*pose* it is.

JILL: Think how lucky we are. There—you look better already!

JACK: Then I *was* looking awful!

JILL: No! Have another? Mills! Two more.

(*Pause.*)

JACK: Not many blokes here.

JILL: Busy time of year.

(*Pause.*)

JILL: *I* had rather a successful week.

JACK: Oh?

JILL: In fact, what you might call triumphant.

JACK: That's nice for you.

JILL: Yes.

(*Pause.*)

JILL: Shall we go down? I ordered for eight.

JACK: I haven't had this other drink yet.

JILL: Ah, no.

JACK: I'm sorry I can't swallow these things right down like you can.

JILL: No.

JACK: I'll leave it if you like.

JILL: No, please take your time.

JACK: I didn't know there was a rush on.

JILL: There's no hurry at all. The table will wait.

(*She looks at her watch. Pause.*)

JACK: You did say we had all evening.

JILL: We have, my darling. We have.

(*She smiles at him as he sips his drink very slowly.*)

JACK: Do they have any olives here?

JILL: Sure. Mills!

JACK: Oh, don't bother. I just thought I fancied some.

JILL: Then you shall. Mills!

JACK: I say, you are good.

(*He touches her hand, then looks around the room curiously.*)

INT. CLUB DINING ROOM NIGHT

JILL and JACK at table. She is talking to the WAITER *while* JACK *looks unconcernedly round the room.*

JILL: Ah yes, I forgot. You've decanted the claret. Then we'll have the '69 now. All right, darling?

JACK: What? Oh, you know me. Don't know one from another.

(JILL *nods and the* WAITER *opens and pours a bottle of champagne, which she approves.*)

JILL: Well, then, that's all done.

JACK: What's done?

JILL: Let's talk about you.

JACK (*interested*): Oh, nothing really. I did those two weeks at Watford but I wasn't right for the part, the director hated my guts, none of the London Press bothered to come and the weather kept the customers away to say nothing of the play. I didn't get that modelling job for pipe tobacco which I was depending on to pay for the jacket.

JILL: Won't you let me——

JACK: No, it's smashing of you but you know what I feel about that. So then I had this almighty row with my father about getting a proper job as he calls it and then Leeds went and lost at home two nil . . .

21. EXT. CLUB ENTRANCE NIGHT

Rain pouring.

JACK: It's worse if anything.

JILL: At least it's warmer. Now you stay there in the warm. Won't be a minute.

(*She dashes into the rain and disappears down the street while* JACK *huddles in the warm portals of the club.*)

22. EXT. CLUB NIGHT

JILL's car draws up. She gets out, opens an umbrella and rushes over to the club entrance and ushers the waiting JACK into the car. She whips round beside him and starts up the car.

JILL: There! That wasn't so bad.
JACK: Depends on your point of view.
JILL: Now for a nice warming drink.

23. INT. JILL'S SITTING ROOM NIGHT

She is standing by the fireplace. He is sitting.

JILL: Another?
JACK: No thanks. I must go in a minute . . .
JILL: I'm sorry if I upset you.
JACK: You didn't. I'm jolly flattered.
JILL: Please, will you, stay the night? Just as usual.
JACK: I'm sorry, darling. But I don't feel like it tonight. And I seem to be having one of my odd spells at the moment. . . . You see, I, I never expected you to bring up marriage . . .
JILL: I know. I did rather spring it . . .
JACK: Do you love me for *myself*? Why should you pay for *me*? My beer money, clothes? You see. . . . Well—marriage.
JILL: I know. It was a mistake. Forget it.
JACK: I can't. You know I love you. But——
JILL: Marriage . . .
JACK: And it isn't just career and all those things. One can arrange all that if you're intelligent. But, well, I know I'll never get into the Big League—in anything—not like you——
JILL: Oh, come.
JACK: As for children. Well, I quite like my nieces and other people's.

JILL: But looking after them yourself.
JACK: Well, you know what nannies are like. You're at *their* mercy and it's someone else in the house . . . babysitting, growing up, education, all that. And it goes on for so *long*. I mean small babies are all right but they do grow and who knows what. You should see Mark's nephew. He's *gruesome* and only fourteen. Fourteen years of that.
JILL: We needn't——
JACK: No. I know how you really feel. And some time it would come up. Bound to.
JILL: I'm sorry . . .
JACK: So am I . . . I'd better go——
JILL: I'll take you to the station.
JACK: It's not much of a place. But it's mine and *I* like it . . . Mark and I get on pretty well. . . . He has *his* girls and I—Oh, my darling.
(*They embrace passionately.*)
I expect you've got to get up at dawn.
JILL: More or less.
JACK: At least I can lie in. I'm playing squash in the afternoon. Let me get a cab. Please.
JILL: No, you won't.
(*She touches his lips. They embrace again.*)

24. EXT. RAILWAY STATION NIGHT

JILL *and* JACK *dash from the car.* JACK *can't find his ticket. She buys him one, while he fusses over his overnight case with the ticket collector at the barrier. She finally gets him on to the leaving train, kissing him quickly, then watching the train disappear. She slowly walks back down the platform to her car.*

25. INT. JILL'S BEDROOM NIGHT

She is changing into a very dashing dressing gown over her night clothes and MARY *knocks and enters.*
MARY: Hullo. Alone?

JILL: Yes. All alone.

MARY: How'd it work out?

JILL: What they call 'all for the best' I dare say. You?

MARY: Oh. He had to get up early and didn't get any sleep last night—dancing the night away.

JILL: And the evening?

MARY: Nobody noticed him.

WILLIE: Nobody noticed him!

JILL: Shut up, Willie. I've had enough tonight.

MARY: Tell me, if it's not impertinent: how was he in the sack?

JILL: Not much.

MARY: I know. But thought he was great.

JILL: Right.

MARY: Oh, well, back to the address book.

JILL: I can do without, thanks. All for what?

MARY: Maybe you're right. Soldier on a bit, perhaps. 'Night. Sweet dreams.

JILL: 'Night.

MARY: Men . . .

(*She goes out.*)

WILLIE: Men!

(JILL *picks up her brief-case and opens papers on to her desk.*)

JILL: Who needs 'em.

WILLIE: Who needs 'em!

(MARY *looks in the door.*)

MARY: You won't let Willie chatter on about *him*self, will you? I've an early start!

(JILL *goes to the bathroom to put cloth over* WILLIE's *cage.*)

JILL: So have I.

WILLIE: So have I! Men! So have I!

MARY: Do you think it was because he's an actor?

JILL: No. Not at all. He was self-involved; vain; out of touch with everything except his own deficiencies.

MARY: Yes. I suppose so.

JILL: Also——

MARY: What?

JILL: He had NO . . . INNER . . . LIFE—that's all.

78

MARY: Well, you've shut up the bird.
JILL: It's not difficult.
(MARY *goes out.* JILL, *at her desk, puts on her spectacles and switches on a record. The parrot is quiet in his darkened cage.*)

THE END